Praise for *Beyond Jesus*

"Staying humbly within her own experience, Pearce has addressed a larger story that is unfolding from the edge of Christianity. The countless Christians' journey 'beyond Jesus' is now a much larger. culture-wide odyssey, and needs the close attention Pearce brings to it in order to understand its significance."

—THE REV. DR. HAL TAUSSIG, National Co-Chair, Christianity Seminar, Westar Institute, and editor of *A New New Testament: A Bible for the 21st Century Combining Traditional and Newly Discovered Texts*

"Patricia Pearce's spiritual odyssey illuminates the wisdom and light that shine within us all. She asserts that this power, the greatest power, is the incredible, immense force of love in the universe that connects all beings to one another in the amazing web of Life. Thank you, Patricia Pearce, for walking this path and sharing it with the rest of us."

—KATHRYN "KITSI" WATTERSON, author of *I Hear My People Singing: Voices of African American Princeton, Not by the Sword,* and *Women in Prison: Inside the Concrete Womb*

"This is the very personal journey of an earnest Western seeker out to rescue what Marcus Borg, John Dominic Crossan, and others have called the 'Jesus of history,' the God-conscious human being who survived his early and brutal execution by the Roman state. A useful guide for any of us today who are looking for a life, as she says, 'freed from the ego and its illusions.'"

—MICHAEL NAGLER, PHD, founder of the Metta Center for Nonviolence and author of *The Search for a Nonviolent Future*

"Halfway through the introduction, I was in tears. Pearce's sharing of how her individual journey meshed with the universal seeking for God and the commitment to act for justice in ways that honor the God-spark dignity of all life forms of our planet moved me into and beyond the words of her life story. Beyond words, into tears—and joy."

—RABBI ARTHUR WASKOW, author of *Godwrestling—Round 2* and director of The Shalom Center

Beyond Jesus

My Spiritual Odyssey

Patricia A. Pearce

swp

SHE WRITES PRESS

Also by Patricia Pearce

No One in I Land: A Parable of Awakening

Published July 3, 2018
Printed in the United States of America
Print ISBN: 978-1-63152-359-5
E-ISBN: 978-1-63152-360-1
Library of Congress Control Number: 2017957972

For information, address:
She Writes Press
1563 Solano Ave #546
Berkeley, CA 94707

Cover and interior design by Tabitha Lahr

She Writes Press is a division of SparkPoint Studio, LLC.

In Memory of Tricia—
whose life, love, and death
changed me

1. Introduction

Jesus has become an obstacle to our spiritual evolution—not because of who he was but because of who we have made him out to be. Viewing Jesus as "the one and only Son of God," we deny our own divine nature and distance ourselves from the Christ consciousness accessible to us all. Not only is this projection of our divine essence onto a solitary individual unhelpful, it is the antithesis of the message Jesus was attempting to impart.

This issue was brought home to me one morning when I was still a pastor. I was alone in the sanctuary rehearsing the gospel story I had memorized for our upcoming Sunday worship—a story about Jesus's disciples arguing with one another about who among them was the greatest. Jesus called them together and, attempting to convey the essence of his teaching, took a child in his arms and said, "Whoever welcomes one such child in my name welcomes me, and whoever welcomes me welcomes not me but the one who sent me."

As I told the story aloud in the vacant sanctuary, I was suddenly overwhelmed by a tremendous grief. The odd thing was, the grief didn't seem to belong to me. It seemed to flow from a source beyond me, and the words in the story that triggered it and kept repeating themselves over and over in my mind, were, "Not me. Not me. Not me." The magnitude of the grief drove me to my knees.

I felt in that moment that I had become an available vessel for a great sorrow—sorrow that the religion born in Jesus's name had come to be focused not upon what he wanted to impart, but upon him.

Whether my experience in the sanctuary that day was a transcendent encounter or simply a realization breaking forth from the depths of my own psyche isn't important. In either case, it speaks to something my own spiritual journey has led me to believe: when Christianity makes Jesus the point, it misses Jesus's point.

Christian tradition has typically viewed the gospel story I was reciting as a morality lesson: we should concern ourselves, as Jesus did, with the welfare of the vulnerable. But I no longer believe he was giving a morality lesson or was speaking figuratively when he took that child in his arms and in essence said, "This is me." I believe that such was the state of Jesus's consciousness. He did not experience any separation between himself and the child. He knew he *was* the child, the child *was* him.

In the absence of separateness there is no such thing as specialness, which is why the disciples' argument about which of them was the greatest was meaningless. They were caught in the delusions of ego, which sees itself as separate and hungers to be special—precisely the delusion from which Jesus freed himself when he came to see his true—*our* true—nature.

However, this argument about who was the greatest not only continued; it eventually became superimposed upon Jesus himself. For centuries, those who refused to confess that Jesus was the greatest among us suffered unspeakable consequences at the hands of inquisitors and kings. Christianity, in other words, came to be shaped by the beliefs and values of the ego consciousness Jesus was urging us to abandon.

If we consider Jesus to be a doorway, as many people do, then we must ask: What is he a doorway to? One does not stop at a doorway, nor fixate upon it. One moves through it to the other side. That is its purpose.

When we focus our spiritual journey on Jesus himself—when we stop at the doorway—we fail to see what he was showing us about *our own* nature. We abdicate the power he was demonstrating it was possible to attain when we shed the limited and limiting ego. We deprive ourselves of the beautiful and ecstatic experience of our own oneness with Ultimate Reality.

Jesus was able to be a conduit for divine purposes because he himself had moved beyond Jesus. He had moved beyond the narrow confines of a particular identity and into the full realization that he—that *we*—were and always had been one with the Source of Being.

I believe it is both possible and essential that we do the same, because only in the light of awakened consciousness can the collective nightmare of the ego and its empires ever dissolve.

This book is written as a memoir. In the pages to follow, I share a bit about my upbringing in mainstream Protestantism, the events that led me to seminary and then the ministry, and the spiritual awakenings that caused me to see Jesus in a new light—epiphanies that ultimately made it impossible for me to stay in the institutional church.

It also tells the story of how my spirituality has been deeply influenced by what I have witnessed in the political realm. From the impoverished regions of the Andes, where

I served as a Peace Corps Volunteer, to the federal prison where I served a sentence for nonviolent civil disobedience when the United States invaded Iraq, I have seen how our political systems are an outward manifestation of the beliefs we hold about who we are and about the nature of reality. As our consciousness matures, those systems will also undergo a profound change.

While this book is written as a memoir, it is also a manifesto pointing to what we might become. Each of our lives is a hologram, holding the patterns of the evolution of our collective existence, so while the details of any life story are particular, the narrative arc is one we share. We are participating in a great unfolding on this planet, the emergence of a new consciousness that sees through the fallacy of separateness. As the beliefs of a previous age dissolve and the structures and institutions spawned by those beliefs crumble, a new world will become possible, one in which we take our place as co-creators in a cosmos awakening to itself.

This book is an offering to the emergence of that new world—to the great flowering of our spiritual potential that Jesus demonstrated, and the promise it holds for our collective future.

Chapter 1: The Watershed

I grew up in Colorado where the Continental Divide runs through the Rocky Mountains, separating the watershed of the Atlantic from the watershed of the Pacific. Along the Divide all it takes is a single gust of wind to blow a snow-flake from one side to the other. When spring comes and the snowflake melts, it either flows west toward the Colorado River and the Pacific or east toward the Mississippi and the Gulf of Mexico.

The gust of wind that changed the course of my life began with a phone call. It was a Saturday.

"Hello?"

"Hi, Patrish." Gwen's voice was trembling. "Tricia's brain is bleeding and the doctors can't do anything to stop it."

I held the phone to my ear, stunned, unable to believe what I was hearing.

"She's in a coma. They don't expect her to live more than a day or two."

This couldn't be. Tricia's recovery from her bone mar-row transplant had been going so well. Her return to the hospital had just been a little setback. Yesterday, when I had gotten the news, I had been too busy trying to scrub the grime from between our bathroom floor tiles to call her. I planned to do it later. I realized now, to my horror, that later was too late.

Tricia had been my lifeline in seminary during a time of deep struggle. We had accompanied one another through seasons of painful spiritual wilderness. She understood me better than anyone I had ever met. I couldn't imagine my life without her.

She was in the hospital at Stanford. I was living in Philadelphia and had to lead the worship service at my church the next day, so I bought a plane ticket to California for Monday in hopes that she would hang on until I got there.

I got to Stanford Hospital Monday evening. Tricia's family and close friends were standing in the hallway outside her door, taking turns saying their private good-byes to her. When it was my turn, I lay down beside her in the hospital bed and cradled her body against mine.

"Tricia, it's me, Patrish." I felt the warmth of her body. "I want you to know how much I love you. I'm going to miss you so much. But I believe our love is strong enough to bridge the chasm between life and death."

Could she comprehend anything I was saying? Did she even know I was here?

"There's a hymn I wrote about how we're all children of the universe 'created by the Force that hurled this flaming galaxy upon its spinning course.' I'd like to sing it for you."

I leaned in close to her ear and sang.

After I finished the song I held her quietly. I hoped something I had said or sung had been able to penetrate the curtain of her coma. Then I kissed her on the temple, got up and left the room.

In the wee hours of the morning, I returned to the hospital. I walked down the quiet corridor, past the rooms of sleeping patients, until I arrived at Tricia's room, where Tricia's husband, Stephen, and Gwen were sitting vigil.

Gwen looked relieved when I walked in. "Her breathing changed during the night," she told me. "I was hoping you would come quickly."

I sat down with them at her bedside. As dawn approached, another of Tricia's friends arrived and the four of us sat with her, telling stories and singing songs. When the first sunlight lit up the red brick wall of the adjacent hospital wing, a pair of mourning doves landed in a tree just outside the window. They cooed as Tricia's breathing became more labored and intermittent.

When I sensed the time was near, I disentangled my fingers from hers and let her hand rest in my open palm, hoping she would understand the meaning of the gesture. It was okay. She could let go now. Her long fight was over.

Her breathing became more intense, her eyes opened briefly and looked upward, her head lifted slightly. With tears streaming down my face, I told her, "You go, girl! You go, girl!" Then I laid my forehead down on the bed. She was gone.

Chapter 2: When I Was a Child

I cannot explain how, in that crowded room on our first day at San Francisco Theological Seminary, I knew I wanted to be Tricia's friend the moment I saw her. I cannot explain how it was that we were carrying matching gray Land's End bags, or that we shared the same name: Patricia Ann. I cannot explain our mutual love of horses, or how life gave us each other to explore the mysteries of our dreams and accompany one another through the wilderness. What I can say is that our paths to seminary couldn't have been more different.

Tricia grew up in a family of atheists. As an adult she considered whether she would rather live in a world where there was no God or a world in which there was. She decided on the latter, and so her faith journey began.

I, on the other hand, was born to a churchgoing family, and to me the existence of God was a given. My father's ancestry was Scottish, so we were Presbyterians. We went to church every Sunday and said grace before dinner. My mother kept a white leather-bound Bible and the book of daily devotionals she read before saying her prayers every night on her bedside table. But in my family faith was considered a private matter and never spoken of at home, so most of what I learned about God and Jesus I learned at church.

We were members of Central Presbyterian Church in Denver, the oldest Presbyterian church in the city. Its late-1800s red sandstone building stood just a block from the state capitol. On sunny days golden light would stream through the Tiffany windows, illuminating the sanctuary's high arched ceiling and ornate organ pipes, and the brass railings that lined the theater-like box seats. It was there that I was baptized as an infant, though of course I don't remember it.

As a young child I spent most Sunday mornings in Sunday School, but on the rare occasions when I stayed with my parents in worship I always felt exceedingly small. My legs dangled off the edge of the wooden pew while the pipe organ thundered majestic music and the black-robed pastors droned on in their solemn, commanding baritone voices. I have no recollection of anything any of them said. What I remember is the feel of it, of being dwarfed by the power and majesty of the setting, excruciatingly bored by the sermons and prayers, and, though I would not become conscious of it until many years later, rendered irrelevant by the overwhelming maleness of it all.

While worship attested to the power and majesty of God the Father, Sunday School was more like Jesus, God's friendly, approachable counterpart. In Sunday School all the tables and chairs were just the right size for me, and we sang songs like "John Jacob Jingleheimer Schmidt," "Jesus Loves the Little Children," "Zacchaeus Was a Wee Little Man," and "Jesus Loves Me."

There was never any doubt in my mind that Jesus loved me, mostly because of my experience of Mrs. Heter, his stand-in. She was my Sunday School teacher, and every

Sunday when my mother delivered me to her room, she bubbled over with enthusiasm at my arrival. I figured if God was anything like her we were in very good hands.

Every summer I went to church camp in the mountains for a week. One day, while we were all standing outside in a big circle holding hands for our morning prayers, one of the counselors encouraged us to silently invite Jesus into our hearts. I did, and was disappointed when nothing seemed to happen.

I also went to Vacation Bible School every summer, where we did crafts, sang songs, memorized scripture passages, and tried to pulverize each other in dodge ball.

One summer, for our craft project, we made crosses out of partially burned wooden matches that we pasted to a piece of covered plywood. That accomplished, our teacher told us to find a scripture passage to write down next to the cross.

When I was finished, I showed my project to my teacher. I immediately sensed her discomfort, and knew I had done something wrong. It seemed to have to do with the verse I had chosen, which I had thought was ideal: "If you are the Son of God, come down from the cross."

Later on my mother asked me about it—"Why did you choose that verse?" I could tell she was a bit troubled.

I knew by now I was treading on sensitive ground— though I didn't know why—so I gave her a simple answer. "Because it had the word 'cross' in it."

But I didn't tell her my real reason: telling Jesus to come down from the cross seemed like a no-brainer to me, and frankly I couldn't understand why the adults were so uptight about it. Crucifixion seemed like a lousy way to go, and everybody knew he was the *Son of God*, after all, so why shouldn't he?

That was the first time I realized that there must be certain beliefs about Jesus that you weren't supposed to cross, so to speak.

When I was probably eight or nine we had a guest preacher one Sunday, a visiting missionary, and all the children stayed with their parents to hear him instead of going to Sunday School. I don't remember what he talked about, except that at one point he addressed the children directly.

"Children, I have something important I'm going to ask you, and I want you to think seriously about your answer. If God ever called you—if He ever asked you to give your life to Him—would you say 'yes'? If so, I'd like you to please stand."

I hoped one of the other kids would go first, but nobody budged. I knew it was a serious question that deserved an honest response, so I searched my heart until I knew my answer. Finally, overcoming my shyness, I stood up, feeling resolved yet embarrassed that so many adults were looking at me. That's the first time I remember making a deliberate choice to take my relationship with God seriously.

By far my favorite church experience was our Christmas Eve candlelight service. The sanctuary was always decorated with garlands and poinsettias. We sang Christmas carols, listened to the story of Jesus's birth, and celebrated God coming to earth in the form of a little baby to save us from our sins.

At the end we sang "Silent Night" while the flame from the Christ candle was passed among us—a growing sea of candlelight illuminating the sanctuary with a holy glow.

When I reached early adolescence I went through confirmation, which to be honest I don't remember very clearly. As I recall we met in the pastor's office for several weeks as he explained the basics of the faith to us. One Sunday we stood up in front of the congregation to affirm that we accepted Jesus Christ as our Lord and Savior, then took communion for the first time.

My clearest memory of the whole thing was my embarrassing moment during communion. When the elder handed me the silver tray full of tiny glasses of grape juice I picked up one of the cups and drank it, but when I put it back in the tray I saw to my horror that I hadn't drunk it all. The glass was still half full, and I didn't know the protocol in a situation like this. Should I pick it up again and finish drinking it, or was this a one-shot deal and I had blown it?

The kid next to me started to giggle about it, which made me giggle nervously too. The elder, towering over me in his dark suit and tie, scowled at us for our irreverence during such a sacramental moment. I ended up leaving the glass in the tray, but later worried that somebody else might have picked it up and gotten my germs when they thought they were just getting the blood of Christ.

By the time I reached high school, white flight to the suburbs had taken its toll on most downtown churches in Denver, ours included, and there were only a handful of us left who had gone through Sunday School and Vacation Bible School together. We had a small youth group that took occasional ski trips and other excursions, and I kept going to church with my parents, but my church participation began to fade, and soon I was leaving home for college.

Chapter 3: Shattered Innocence

It was 1976 when I enrolled in the University of Colorado in Boulder. Saigon had fallen the year before, and with the war over and nothing else to protest yet, life on campus was pretty quiet.

Other than the few weekends when I was back home, I never went to church, except for the Mass I would occasionally attend with a Catholic friend, where I always felt like an interloper.

The most noticeable presence of religion in my life had to do with a couple of old high school friends. They had gone through their rebellious pot-smoking phase in high school, but when they came to CU they found Jesus, and they wanted me to find him too. Whenever we ran into each other on campus they tried to persuade me to come to their campus Christian group. Their sparkling eyes radiated such born-again bliss that I could have sworn they were still high—now it was just on something they didn't have to smoke. I always found a way to gracefully decline their invitations. I found their transformation unsettling, but

I was also put off by their smugness. They seemed to see themselves as part of an elite group—the Saved—and all the rest of us as poor, wandering, lost souls. Determined to steer clear of whatever spell they had come under, I began avoiding them. Over time our friendship faded.

Since music had always been an important part of my life—I had started playing the French horn when I was in the fourth grade and had continued through high school—and since I didn't have any other ideas about what to do with my life, a degree in music education seemed as good a choice as any.

My sophomore year, some of my classmates in the school of music started telling me I ought to go to West Germany as an exchange student. For several years in a row, one horn student from CU had spent their junior year abroad in Regensburg and played with the university's orchestra. I had taken a few classes in German, so my friends thought I was the logical choice to carry on the tradition.

By some miracle, I sold my parents on the idea.

I didn't tell them that the real reason I wanted to go to Germany had nothing to do with carrying on the music school's tradition—in fact, I never shared my real reason with anybody. But the truth is, I wanted to go because for as long as I could remember I had been gripped by the Holocaust.

I don't recall when I first learned about the Holocaust. Not having grown up in an anti-Semitic family, nothing about it made sense. When we read *The Diary of Anne Frank* in school and learned about the concentration camps in our history class, I found it all unfathomable. How could such a horrific genocide have happened as recently as my own parents' lifetimes?

In tenth grade, when we were learning how to write research papers, my classmates investigated topics like the

Colorado Gold Rush and the rise of the Beatles in America.
My subject was Adolf Eichmann.

Growing up, I didn't know any Jews personally. All I
knew was what I had learned from the Bible and church:
the Jews were God's chosen people, Jesus was a Jew, some
Jews had colluded in Jesus's crucifixion, and Jews didn't
believe Jesus was the Messiah. How you got from that to
genocide was beyond me.

I left for West Germany in August of my junior year
hoping to get some answers.

Regensburg is in northern Bavaria and sits on the Dan-
ube River. Having been spared the Allied bombings that
leveled so many German cities during World War II, its
stone bridge dating to Roman times and its medieval buildings still stood, mostly unscathed by the passage of time.

I took classes in history and German literature, played
in the orchestra, and kept my eye out for clues that might
provide answers to my nagging questions. But what I discovered only added to my confusion: the German people were
quite normal. Some of my classmates showed me around,
helped me with my German, took me along with them on
vacations, and invited me home with them for the holidays.

Their kindness left me utterly perplexed. If such normal people could carry out such inhumane acts, then who
was to say it couldn't happen anywhere?

It was the late seventies, and there had still been no
public reckoning in Germany about the Holocaust. So when
the PBS miniseries *Holocaust* was broadcast on national television, it was a historic occasion.

After each episode viewers could dial into a radio
forum to share their feelings. One elderly woman called in
and sobbed as she recounted watching her Jewish neighbors
being taken away in the night. "*Warum habe ich nichts gemacht?*"
she cried over and over again. "Why didn't I do anything?"

Many of my German classmates were struggling, as I was, to make sense of the Third Reich. For them, though, the horror was magnified. It was their own parents and grandparents who had witnessed, and maybe even participated in, the atrocities.

For my part, I had my own explaining to do whenever someone asked me to account for what the United States had done in Vietnam. The war had only recently ended, and the images of torched villages, napalmed children, and self-immolating Buddhist monks were fresh in people's minds. I always found myself on the losing side of those debates, not only because there was no excuse for what we had done but also because of how well-informed my German peers were about international politics.

I went to Berlin on a trip the university organized for exchange students that year. This was during the Cold War, so the city was still divided by the Wall. We mostly toured West Berlin, but we also entered East Berlin a couple of times through Checkpoint Charlie. Since the Wall had been built by the Soviets to prevent people from fleeing to the West, residents of the Eastern Bloc were not permitted to leave; Westerners, though, could visit East Berlin— provided we stayed within a designated perimeter. Going through the checkpoint under the scrutinizing eye of armed Soviet soldiers was chilling, and gave me a taste of what it must be like to live in a police state.

On one of our forays into East Berlin, a friend of mine and I decided to take public transportation as far as we could. We wanted to see what life was like outside the tourist area of downtown East Berlin. We boarded a trolley and rode it to where it ended in a drab neighborhood, and then started exploring.

During our excursion, a couple of young East German soldiers stopped us.

"Where are you from?" one of them asked.

My pulse quickened. Had we transgressed some Soviet law, venturing so far from the designated tourist area?

"Wait, let us guess! Poland?" he asked.

"Hungary?" asked the other.

I realized, relieved, that they weren't questioning us. They were flirting with us. I couldn't help but notice they were only naming countries behind the Iron Curtain.

Julie responded in her Missouri-accented German, "We're Americans!"

"No you're not! Come on. Where are you really from? Romania?"

"No, really, we're Americans," I said. "We're just visiting East Berlin for the day."

When we finally convinced them we were from the US, the conversation soon turned adversarial. Each of us was certain our own political and economic system was superior, and we were determined to prove it.

Julie got things rolling. "Why aren't there any apples in the store?" She pointed over to the meagerly stocked market we had just visited.

I suspected she was trying to point out that communism couldn't deliver the goods, literally. But I was embarrassed by her question. It smacked of ignorance, or worse, entitlement. "We Americans can have whatever we want whenever we want it."

Wanting to demonstrate that Americans could be sensible, I looked at Julie and stated the obvious: "Apples aren't in season."

The soldiers nodded in agreement.

The detente didn't last long, though, once we started talking about uprisings. Julie and I criticized the Soviets' habit of sending in tanks anytime someone challenged their regime.

Then one of the soldiers countered with a question that would change my life: "What about what the United States did in Chile?"

I had no knowledge of anything the United States had done in Chile. We were the good guys. We didn't overthrow democratically elected governments; the Soviets were the ones with imperialist ambitions. We didn't meddle, except for Vietnam—which had been a tragic, misguided exception.

"We never did anything in Chile," I insisted, whereupon the two soldiers looked at each other incredulously and burst out laughing.

That was when the horrifying realization hit me: I had been duped.

As a child I had said the Pledge of Allegiance every day at school. I had dutifully scrambled under my desk during civil defense drills, obedient though skeptical that it would save me in a nuclear attack. I had believed all I had been taught about the Soviet Union—that it was a dangerous, untrustworthy government that spied on its own citizens and brainwashed them with propaganda. Now I was shocked to realize that I, too, had been brainwashed. I felt gullible, foolish, betrayed.

Managing to hide my consternation, I came back at the soldiers with a below-the-belt rebuttal. "If your system is so good, why can't you leave?"

The Berlin Wall said it all. They were prisoners in their own land.

The soldiers looked pained. They had no clever retort. The four of us parted company, but I would never shake the truth the soldiers had revealed.

Chapter 4: A Seed Planted
in the Andes

R iding through the Andes of Ecuador on my way to the town of Guaranda, where I would begin my work as a Peace Corps Volunteer, every now and then the fog would lift enough for me to see the llamas grazing on the páramo hillside and the mammoth, snow-covered peak of Chimborazo towering overhead.

After my experience in Germany, especially my encounter with the soldiers in East Berlin, I'd known I needed to know more about the world and what my country had been up to, so when I returned to Boulder I had taken up a new major: international affairs.

Although it had taken me an extra year to graduate, the degree program had given me the background I had been hoping for. As graduation approached, I had still felt hungry to learn more about the world, and about myself. I decided joining the Peace Corps would help me do both.

As we rumbled along the winding Andean road, every now and then one of the Quichua Indians would ask the driver to stop the bus so he could get off. As his dark blue fedora hat and red woolen poncho disappeared into the fog, I wondered where on earth he was headed and how far he would have to walk to get there.

Four hours southwest of Quito, Guaranda—capital of the "forgotten province"—wasn't on the road to anywhere. Despite the beauty of the hillsides and mountains surrounding it, I found it depressing. Its isolation lay over it like a blanket of despair.

I had been assigned to the Peace Corps' appropriate technology program and had been trained in the construction of passive solar water heating systems. Before I left for Guaranda, my program director and I had signed an agreement with the Ministry of Agriculture stating that I could build a passive solar water heating system on their demonstration farm so people in the area could see what solar was all about. The Ministry had assured me that they would soon be installing the running water on the farm I would need to carry out the project.

As the weeks turned into months and still the Ministry hadn't fulfilled their end of the bargain, I had to accept that the demonstration project was, literally, dead in the water.

If that weren't discouraging enough, as I traveled to surrounding villages to help other Peace Corps Volunteers build adobe wood-burning cookstoves, I saw how most people in the region lived. They had no electricity or running water—many of them were struggling just to survive. The idea of introducing solar water heaters was absurd.

But the hardest thing for me to deal with was the tremendous economic disparity in the country, which hit me especially hard one evening when I traveled to Quito to attend a concert by the New York Philharmonic. I had splurged my meager monthly stipend to buy a ticket.

The Who's Who of Ecuadorian society, including the

president, was in attendance at the concert. As I sat listening to the orchestra play an exquisite rendition of "Pictures at an Exhibition," my mind traveled back to the *campesino* home where I had helped build a cookstove the day before. The family lived in an earthen hut with a dirt floor and thatched roof. The children, their hair slightly red from malnutrition, ran about barefoot because they couldn't afford shoes.

Now, a day later, I was sitting in a red velvet upholstered seat beneath an enormous crystal chandelier, surrounded by men in tuxedos and women shrouded in evening gowns, perfume, and diamonds.

The shocking disparity was the legacy of colonialism. When the Spanish *conquistadores* came to South America in the sixteenth century, they established large *haciendas* where the Quichua were forced to labor as peons or sharecroppers. For three centuries the Quichua had endured humiliating and sometimes brutal treatment at the hands of colonial powers.

On Guaranda's market day, the Quichua came down from the mountains to trade and, in the case of the men, get drunk. One day I was riding the bus back from Quito on market day, and as we drove through town we passed a Quichua woman trying to pull her drunk husband, who was lying in the middle of the street and fondling himself, out of the line of traffic. It was a tableau of despair.

With my degree in international affairs, I had arrived in Ecuador believing that politics, if done right, could solve any problem. But the overwhelming poverty, injustice, and disparity I witnessed there made me think there was something going on there that politics couldn't begin to touch. Some sort of spiritual sickness lay at the root of it all.

I started attending a Bible study for area Peace Corps Volunteers that a missionary couple held—mostly so I could be around people who spoke my language and shared my culture. I was leery of the whole missionary enterprise, and often found myself put off by their literalist approach to the Bible, and yet some of the biblical stories I had been steeped in since my childhood began speaking to me in new and powerful ways.

After a year of spinning my wheels in Guaranda I was feeling discouraged. Harder still, all the other single women volunteers who had come to Ecuador with me had returned home, mostly because of the *machista* culture. When I broke down sobbing in the Quito airport saying good-bye to my best friend there, I started to wonder if I should do the same.

Just as I was seriously considering leaving, an agronomist from the US invited me to come work with him. Phil wanted to start up a project building potato silos in remote Quichua communities. Potatoes were one of the major crops of the Quichua, and the silos, which he had seen in Bolivia, would keep their seed potatoes healthy, boosting their harvests.

Phil didn't have time to oversee the project and wanted a Peace Corps Volunteer to take it over. I decided to give it a go.

I moved to the small Quichua village of Colta in Chimborazo Province. At an altitude of nearly 10,500 feet, Colta sat next to the Pan-American Highway, a two-lane road running north to south through the country. On the other side of the "highway" was a large lake. The steep hillsides surrounding the valley were dotted with a patchwork of cultivated plots of mostly potatoes and barley, and at the upper elevations, which were too high for agriculture, the Quichua grazed their sheep on the wild páramo grasses. At the north end of the valley loomed Chimborazo's spectacular peak.

I had already heard about Colta long before moving there. In an overwhelmingly Catholic nation, it was a region that had become mostly evangelical Protestant. Decades earlier, a young missionary woman from North America had come down and settled in the village. She had learned the language and spent the rest of her life there, even though not a single Quichua converted during her lifetime. After she retired more missionaries arrived, and slowly the Quichua in the region began to adopt the newcomers' evangelical faith.

I felt ambivalent about it all. It seemed to me one more form of colonialism. I was also troubled by the large houses the missionaries lived in, which, although basic by North American standards, were palatial compared to Quichua dwellings.

On the other hand, I could see how dedicated the missionaries were to the Quichua, giving up a more comfortable life with their family and friends back home. And it was undeniable that some aspects of the Quichua's lives had improved. Alcoholism and domestic violence—huge problems elsewhere—were rare in Colta.

Most Quichua homes were one-room, earthen huts with a thatched roof. Newer houses, like the one I lived in, were made of bare cinder block walls and tin roofs. My living quarters consisted of two rooms on the second floor of a small house. The first floor was used for storage for Phil's projects. When I arrived electricity was just being installed in the village, and my house had a bare light bulb and an outlet in each room.

There was no running water. I carried my water from a public well and boiled it before using it so it would be safe to drink. Communal pit latrines had been built inside the missionary compound, but since the compound was locked up at night, and since my house was too close to my neighbor's well for me to build a latrine, one of the missionaries loaned me her camping toilet.

It was a simple life, and I found it freeing to discover how little I actually needed. Every night, brushing my teeth on the small balcony that adjoined my two rooms, I looked out at a sky filled with stars and the majestic sight of Chimborazo lit up by the moonlight.

My responsibilities with the silo project were to oversee the funding and purchase of materials, keep an inventory of supplies, and arrange for delivery of materials to the far-reaching communities. Phil felt strongly that each village needed to be invested in their community silo, so although we received some grant money to subsidize costs, each community contributed money and labor.

Many times I rode along in the truck that delivered materials to the villages. We often traveled for hours over rutted, muddy roads that were barely passable, especially during the rainy season. When we got stuck we would climb out and shove rocks under the muddy wheels to try to get traction. Miraculously, we always managed to get to our destination, where we were invariably welcomed with a meal of boiled potatoes and warm Coke.

By now I had become pretty fluent in Spanish, although in many cases it didn't do me much good. The native language, Quichua, was the only language many of the people, especially the women, spoke. Since I worked with men—who were usually conversant in Spanish—I got by, but after a short time in Colta I asked one of the young bilingual women to tutor me in Quichua so I could at least carry on a rudimentary conversation.

The missionaries had recently finished translating the New Testament into Quichua, but it seemed the Quichua often understood the message better than the North Americans. Their lives, after all, weren't much different from those of the people of Jesus's day. For centuries they too had struggled to survive as subsistence farmers under an oppressive imperial system.

Not only that, but many of Jesus's parables drew on agricultural activities that were part of their daily lives. They plowed their fields with oxen. They knew how much concentration and strength it required, and that anybody who looked backwards while doing it was a fool. They knew about sowing seeds by hand—how some inevitably landed on rocky ground while others landed on fertile soil. As children, many of them had been shepherds, taking their family's sheep out to pasture early each day and bringing them back at sundown. They knew how vulnerable sheep were, how much they needed guidance and protection.

While the missionaries' primary concern seemed to be saving souls, the Quichua were very focused on the here and now. They were at the lowest rung of Ecuador's socioeconomic ladder, and they heard a revolutionary message in the gospels: they were loved by God. Despite their poverty and the discrimination they faced, they had inherent human dignity.

Their empowering encounter with the gospel caused the Quichua to become increasingly intolerant of the dehumanizing treatment they often received, and they set about doing something about it. Partnering with the missionaries, they started a savings and loan, a seed cooperative, and eventually, because of the humiliating treatment they were subjected to whenever they rode the bus to market, even their own bus line.

Despite the improvements they had made, however, life for the Quichua was difficult.

One day I got a startling glimpse into the deep resignation that had taken root within so many of them. I was visiting my friend José in his hut, talking with him and his adult son, Pedro, who was fiddling with a tape measure. A heavy rain began outside and suddenly there was a flash of light. Pedro screamed and fell backward. Lightning had struck, jumping from the light socket overhead to the outlet on the wall. Pedro, holding the metal tape measure, was directly in its path.

José had only one eye. He had lost the other as a young man when he was hit by a machete while harvesting sugarcane on the coast. His remaining eye was also badly damaged, leaving him nearly blind.

As his son lay motionless on the floor, José turned to me and quietly asked, "*¿Señorita, está muerto?*" Señorita, is he dead?

The fatalism in his voice jolted me as much as the lightning strike had. José had experienced so much misfortune in his life—the loss of a baby daughter, the loss of his eyesight, the loss of much of his land. He had come to expect tragedy.

Pedro was only stunned.

"*No, José. Está vivo.*" He is alive. As José bent down to touch him, Pedro screamed at him not to, warning him that another strike could be coming.

In the US we have a saying that lightning never strikes twice. The Quichua had the opposite belief: if lightning has struck once, it is likely to strike again. Fortunately it didn't, and after a few days Pedro made a full recovery.

The missionaries held a weekly Bible study, which I started to attend, and Phil loaned me his copy of C. S. Lewis's book *Mere Christianity*. One evening I came to a chapter titled "The Great Sin." Reading Lewis's description of the vice he said all people have, though few admit it—pride—I had a shocking awareness. I suddenly saw how, deep down, I had always harbored an unconscious belief that I was better than other people. Pride had formed an impenetrable barrier between me and God.

As the wall of denial within me collapsed, I was filled with remorse. Yet in the same instant I was flooded with the awareness that I had always been held in God's unconditional love. I was already completely forgiven.

Shaken, I set the book down and walked out into the chilly night. This was the answer to the question that had hounded me throughout my time in Ecuador. The spiritual sickness that was at the root of the oppression and injustice I had been witnessing was pride. All of the exploitation arose from this erroneous belief people held that they were better than others. I was shocked to realize that all along this same sickness had been hiding within me as well.

I walked down the narrow dirt road, past the silent huts and sleeping livestock. I crossed the deserted highway and stood on the lakeshore. The water was still, the starry night peaceful.

Something life-changing had just happened to me. I could feel it. An old self had fallen away, and something new was taking its place.

In the following weeks I felt inwardly light, filled with gratitude. The world seemed more vibrant. I felt more alive. I understood now what people meant when they talked about being born again.

I started reading the Bible from beginning to end, using the study materials one of the missionaries had given me. The interpretations presented in the materials were so clear-cut, so straightforward, that I found myself persuaded by their literal viewpoint.

A few months later, my two and a half years in Ecuador

drew to a close. The potato silo project had exceeded our expectations: Phil had estimated we would build ten or fifteen silos, but after a year and a half we had built sixty-five. Unlike the frustrating experience I had had in Guaranda, the silos were a technology the people actually wanted.

Shortly before I returned home, I was visiting one of the missionaries one day and he asked me, "Why don't you go back to the States, go to Bible college, and come back and join us?"

I was touched by his invitation, but I didn't take it seriously. Although my time in Ecuador had been meaningful, I didn't want to spend the rest of my life there, nor did I want to become a missionary. But his suggestion that I go into ministry landed in my heart like a seed in fertile soil.

Chapter 5: Following the Call

The plane touched down in Miami and taxied to the gate. When I stepped out of the jetway and into the spacious, well-lit, carpeted terminal, I couldn't believe my eyes. There were rows of comfortable chairs, phone kiosks, drinking fountains, shops selling high-tech products, and voices coming over the PA speaking *English.*

I wandered through the airport, dazed and amazed, until it was time to catch my connecting flight to Denver.

In Denver, the shock continued. My parents picked me up at the airport. As we drove across town we passed the most opulent sights imaginable—sleek concrete overpasses, swanky shopping malls, and single-family homes, each with their own manicured yard and multiple cars in the driveway.

Walking into my childhood home, I was stunned by its luxuriousness: upholstered furniture, wall-to-wall carpeting, drapes, a refrigerator, stereo, televisions, indoor plumbing. Hot running water!

I was seeing our middle-class lifestyle through different eyes. Juxtaposed with the poverty I had witnessed in Ecuador, I found it unsettling.

I had experienced reverse culture shock before, returning from Germany. I hadn't been prepared for home no longer feeling like home, for the fact that my time overseas had changed me and that the people I had been close to had no way of understanding what I had experienced and sometimes didn't know how to relate to me. It had been an intensely lonely experience. At least this time I knew what to expect.

I began teaching high school Spanish and English as a Second Language, taking classes in the evenings for a master's in education. I also returned to my home church—but just like the culture around me, it seemed alien. Compared to the faith commitment I had experienced among the missionaries and the Quichua, the Christianity of my Denver church seemed far too tame.

The people at Central Presbyterian Church, though, had known me since I was born. They'd seen me grow up and go off to college. They'd encouraged me and prayed for me when I went into the Peace Corps. I had deep roots there. So even though I was in a different place spiritually, I continued going. Before long I joined the choir, and the young adult group.

One Sunday the Young Adults were having a lesson on Paul's letter to the Romans. I was eager to show off my knowledge—after all, I had read the Bible cover to cover—so when our pastor, John, asked us what Paul's letter was about I confidently chimed in. When I was done, John very graciously let me know that my interpretation was a bit simplistic.

When the class was over, one of the young women approached John and I overheard her ask him, "Why do people who've been saved become so self-righteous?"

"I don't know," he said. "It's puzzling. But it seems to happen more often than not."

Although I knew her question wasn't about me, when I heard it I felt mortified. It was like she'd held up a mirror to me, and I was horrified by what I saw. Ever since I had come back from Ecuador I had believed I knew God better than the people around me. Obviously, my pride had made a spectacular comeback.

I found out that John taught a yearlong class on the Bible, and I signed up for it. In the course, we didn't study the Bible as the inerrant word of God, as the missionaries had; rather, we read it as the journey of a people seeking to be in right relationship with God. The scriptures were rich stories that could convey truth, whether or not they were factual. I was skeptical at first, but soon I began to find the approach compelling.

One of our class assignments was to visit a worship service of another congregation. Along with a few class-mates, I signed up to visit Happy Church, an up-and-coming non-denominational mega-church in Denver.

It was an evening service. We took our seats in the balcony. Before worship started, a praise band played on stage as neatly dressed young families filed into the large, modern sanctuary and took their seats. A palpable, joyous excitement filled the room—the kind of spiritual exuberance I had been missing.

The guest preacher gave a sermon on a passage from the Book of Revelation. Correlating the symbols of the text to current events, he unlocked its hidden meaning.

"What this text is revealing to us is that the Soviets will launch a nuclear attack on the United States, but God will send an electrical storm that will cause the missiles' guidance systems to go haywire. They will rain back down on the Soviet Union and destroy it in a nuclear Armageddon."

Upon hearing this good news, the joyous people of Happy Church cheered wildly.

I was horrified. Was this where religious self-righteousness led? What about Jesus, who taught us to love our enemies and pray for those who persecute us? Did the members of Happy Church actually believe the sermon they had just heard was a Christian teaching?

After the sermon, the preacher led the altar call. "The Spirit is telling me there are some people here who haven't yet been saved. A few people up in the balcony."

He looked up our way.

"Now is the time. Come forward and give your lives to Christ."

We didn't budge. He repeated his plea, and still we didn't budge. Finally he gave up and the service ended.

I stepped out of the church into the night air, shaken. I had just looked religious fundamentalism in the face, and it was frightening. Suddenly I felt deeply grateful for the "tame" version of Christianity we observed at Central.

A few months after my return from Ecuador, our church called a woman named Sue to be our associate pastor. I had never had a woman pastor before, and I was intrigued. Sue, who shared my interest in Latin America, reached out to me, and we began to form a friendship. She was an excellent pastor whom I admired and respected.

But when I got a phone call from a member of the church's nominating committee asking whether I would serve as an elder on the church's governing board I balked. I was still holding on to some of the biblical literalism that had won me over in Ecuador, and I was uncomfortable with the idea of being ordained. I knew what the Bible had to say about women holding leadership in the church.

The longer I sat with the question, though, the more confused I became. The Bible said women shouldn't be leaders, but the Bible said a lot of things that we no longer paid attention to. What if, in this case, God was speaking through the people on the nominating committee rather than through centuries-old scriptures?

Finally, I agreed and I was ordained as an elder.

Soon after my ordination, Sue asked if I would chair the Mission and Outreach Commission. She and I both wanted to deepen the congregation's awareness of homelessness and economic disparity, so we organized an "urban plunge" in which several church members spent a weekend living on the streets and staying in shelters. We also organized a trip to the Mexican border so our members could learn more about the struggles of the people living there.

Before we left on our trip to the border, Sue asked if I would give a sermon about it when we returned. I discovered I loved the challenge of connecting scripture with our present-day circumstances, even though standing up in front of the congregation to preach proved nerve-wracking.

Motivated by my position as chair of the Mission and Outreach Commission, I began researching the wars that were going on in Central America. When I learned about the aid, arms, and military training the United States was giving to the regimes in El Salvador and Guatemala, I was filled with outrage. These governments were torturing, killing, and disappearing their citizens—and the US was helping them. I couldn't help but recall the soldiers in East Berlin who had shattered my naiveté about my government and its motives.

But that was only one of the international issues that grieved me. By the mid 1980s, the United States had stockpiled a frightening arsenal of nuclear weapons and was engaged in a deadly game of chicken with the Soviet Union. Once again at Sue's prompting, I signed up for a Faith and

Resistance Retreat to protest the MX missiles that were stored in underground silos across the Midwest.

"The danger in confronting evil is that it can bring out the evil in us," the diminutive Catholic nun standing before the group said.

She was one of many inspiring speakers who were helping to prepare us for an action of civil disobedience at Warren Air Force Base outside Cheyenne, Wyoming. The leaders introduced us to the principles of nonviolence, and then we did role plays about getting arrested so we would know how to respond nonviolently if we were attacked or provoked.

It was up to each of us to decide what part of the resistance we wished to partake in: we could cross the property line of the military base and risk being arrested, or serve on one of the support teams witnessing the action and working on the outside as needed.

I was torn. I was afraid that having an arrest on my record could jeopardize my chances of landing a permanent teaching job, which I was actively seeking. But I also felt that there was something much bigger at stake than my own security. The real question I had to face was whether I was willing to cross the boundary of my own fear.

I finally decided I would participate in the action, inspired in part by Sue's mother, who was also at the retreat.

"Jane, why are you going to take part in the action?" I asked her.

"Well, I'm looking at it as preparation. In case God asks me to do something that takes even more courage in the future."

On a sunny Sunday morning following our training, we gathered on the windswept prairie at the edge of Warren Air Force Base for a time of prayer. Then, in small groups, we approached the property line while our support teams stood nearby as witnesses. Air Force personnel waited on the other side to arrest us.

My group was a small contingent of four. When it was our turn we joined arms, carrying a banner that read *Presbyterians for Peace*, and crossed onto the base singing "Amazing Grace."

Sacramental. That's the only word that adequately describes what the moment felt like to me. Offering myself to a greater purpose despite my fears, I felt I was saying yes to God in a whole new way. I was filled with deep peace.

The Air Force personnel loaded us onto a bus and took us to the main building, where we were frisk-searched, fingerprinted, and photographed. As we were being processed I asked one of the officers, a young African American man, "What do you think of us doing this?"

He looked around and said in a hushed voice, "If I weren't in here, I would be doing the same thing."

The government chose not to press charges. We were sent away with a warning not to set foot on any military property for a year.

As it turned out, I needn't have worried about having an arrest on my record, because after four years back home I decided to leave teaching. The truth is, whenever I thought about my future, I saw myself doing some sort of ministry. I finally decided that if that was the future I saw for myself I might as well get on with it.

Around this same time, some of my friends started asking me if I had ever thought about going to seminary. Apparently I wasn't the only one who saw ministry in my future. But I hadn't yet said anything about it to my mother, and I wasn't looking forward to having the conversation.

Several years earlier, when I told her I was going into the Peace Corps, she had tried to talk me out of it. I expected the same this time. After all, once I left for seminary there was no telling where my path would lead. Chances were slim I would ever live in Denver again.

I drove to my parents' house and found her reading in the living room.

"Mom?" I sat down in the armchair next to her, my stomach fluttering.

"Yes, dear?" She looked up from her reading.

"I'm thinking of going to seminary."

"I'm not surprised."

I was caught off guard, unnerved. Just how long she had seen this coming? Had she just been quietly waiting until I figured it out for myself? Was it possible my mother knew more about my path than I did?

Chapter 6: Earthquakes

I didn't think anything of it when I was studying at my desk and my lamp started to rattle. Since moving to California I had gotten used to it rattling during a tremor. This time, though, it didn't stop. The rattle grew louder and louder and soon my whole room was shaking violently. I ran to the bathroom doorway of my apartment and held onto the doorjamb. The old cinderblock building shook and lurched. I wondered if I was about to die.

It was the fall of my second year at San Francisco Theological Seminary, and the earthquake I was experiencing that evening of October 17, 1989 would turn out to be the largest quake to hit the Bay Area since the Great Earthquake of 1906. It was the perfect metaphor for what my time at SFTS had become.

At first, everything was idyllic. After saying my painful good-byes to family and friends in Denver I headed west across Utah and Nevada, feeling excited about this new adventure. The first night of my drive, I stayed in Salt Lake City. As I pulled out of town at three in the morning to get across the desert before the heat of day, I watched the full moon emerge from a lunar eclipse. Its silver light illuminated the vast salt flats along the deserted highway. God's presence was palpable.

When I finally reached the Bay Area and drove across the Richmond Bridge, the heavy fog I had been driving through since the Sierra Nevada Mountains broke, revealing a crystal blue sky and a breathtaking view of the sparkling San Francisco skyline. White sailboats dotted the glistening bay. Seagulls soared and dipped over the water.

I had never visited the seminary campus, located in San Anselmo in Marin County, and I was wholly unprepared for its beauty. Perched atop a wooded hill, its old stone buildings overlooked a valley in front of Mt. Tamalpais.

I pulled up behind my dorm and parked my car. When I turned off the engine, I heard choral music coming from the top of the hill, and I set out to find it. As I bushwhacked my way through the undergrowth, I startled a small herd of deer, who lifted their tails and bounded off through the trees.

When I got to the top of the hill, I discovered the music had been coming from the seminary chapel, where a worship service was just ending.

This place was magical—and I knew it was exactly where I belonged.

On the first day of orientation, I met Tricia. We were assigned to the same Explorations in Ministry group, in which we would share our faith journeys and support each other through our first year of seminary. It wasn't long before our friendship began to grow roots. We often walked to class, sat, and studied our Hebrew lessons together, and occasionally had breakfast at a local bistro. We spent hours in deep conversation, probing one another's life. Never had I met anyone so insistent on an authentic relationship.

As our coursework began, I discovered that my time

in Ecuador had prepared me in unexpected ways for the program.

"Don't you see?" Dr. Chaney demanded, gesticulating forcefully during his Old Testament lecture. "The Bible is speaking about these injustices!" He was lecturing on *latifundialization*, a process in agrarian times through which the most arable land became concentrated in the hands of the elites who used the peasantry as slave labor to work the land. "This is what the prophets were denouncing! The Bible isn't just a sacred text. It's a political document!"

He was doing his best to convey to his North American, middle-class students the social and economic context in which the Bible was written. For some of my classmates, the idea that the Bible was "political propaganda" was disturbing. But what Dr. Chaney was saying made perfect sense to me. Latifundialization sounded exactly like Latin America's haciendas.

"You're not a Trinitarian if you embrace Arius's ideas! Jesus was the Christ from the beginning, *equal* to the Father."

We were studying heresies in our History of Christianity class. Listening to the discussion, I wanted to scream. All I could think about was my friend Rebecca, lying in an emergency room in a Denver hospital after her most recent suicide attempt—with a gun this time. These theological debates were offensive. With so many hurting souls in the world, why in God's name had the Church spent so much energy for centuries trying to nail down things none of us could ever understand? Who the hell cared how many angels could dance on the head of a pin? The real question was, how could we help heal the hurting people in the world?

I had met Rebecca when she was traveling cross-country and landed in Denver. Her story had emerged piecemeal.

It was months before the truth came out, and years before her darkest memories surfaced. She hadn't simply been making a casual cross-country trip when we met, as it had seemed. She had been running for her life—and eventually, once we got to know each other better, the Pandora's box of abuse she'd suffered at the hands of her father burst open. I was horrified at what she'd had to live through, and astonished at the fortitude and creativity of her psyche.

Knowing Rebecca was now walking the fragile line between life and death made me outraged by our abstract theological arguments, which seemed like an obscene diversion from what really mattered.

And History of Christianity wouldn't be the only course to present me with disturbing challenges my first year.

"He took me to his apartment after our date and raped me!"

Tricia was telling her faith journey in our small Explorations in Ministry group. The way she talked so openly—and with obvious outrage—about her rape astonished me. She wasn't buying into the social stigma that it's the woman who carries the shame of rape. Nor was she going to be silenced by the social taboo that said you weren't supposed to talk about it.

I was awestruck and dismayed by her courage. I knew that when it was my turn I would have to follow her example. She had thrown the windows open wide, and there was no place to hide.

For me, it happened during my junior year of college. I was studying in Germany, and my parents had just flown back home from London after traveling around Europe with me during my spring break. I had decided to use the last couple of weeks to go to Ireland, mostly for the music. I had some friends in Regensburg who had gone there the month before and told me what a great time they'd had. Armed with some suggestions from them on places I could stay, I left London and took the train across England, then caught the ferry to Ireland.

During the journey, I discovered the Irish Sea is not for sissies. The weather was cold and gray, the water relentlessly choppy. As someone prone to seasickness, I was enduring my misery outside on the pitching deck when I noticed something small and shiny lying on the deck. I leaned over to pick it up. It was an Irish penny.

I was instantly enthralled by the penny's beauty. On one side was a bird with long, flowing tail feathers, and on the other an Irish harp. The Irish Sea may be inhospitable, but this penny was extending me a magical welcome to the Emerald Isle. Grateful, I stowed the gift away in my pocket.

When we disembarked in the late afternoon, I caught the bus for Waterford and fell in love with the land on the drive. A rainbow arched over lush pastures where horses grazed, lit up by the late-day sun.

The next day I traveled across the southern coast to Dingle, a sparsely populated peninsula jutting out into the Atlantic Ocean. There I spent a few nights in the home of an old woman who ran a B&B my friends had told me about.

Liza was one of the few native Gaelic speakers still alive, and I spent most of my time sitting around listening to her and her other two guests—there to practice their Gaelic—conversing and making music together. It was magical.

From Dingle I headed north and stopped in one of the coastal towns to spend the night. After checking into a small hotel, I went to a nearby pub for dinner. After I paid and was getting ready to leave, I discovered I had spent the penny I'd picked up on the ferry. Not being a superstitious person, I couldn't understand the feeling of dread that came over me. It was as though I had lost something precious, irreplaceable.

The next day I headed farther up the coast to the town of Doolin, which was known for its music. I got a ride with some guys who assured me I was going to the right place to hear good Irish music. One of them, Seamus, offered to show me around town and take me to the pubs where the best musicians played. After I checked into my B&B, he started giving me the tour, introducing me to some of the locals, including the town's resident "saint," an old man who always blessed everyone and everything.

That evening, we set out to catch some music. I was enthralled by what I heard. The skill of the fiddle, accordion, and tin whistle players weaving their intricate melodies, which were somehow both joyful and melancholy, thrilled me. I was so grateful to be experiencing this music in its native land.

After the show, Seamus asked if I would like to come to a party at his place, and I agreed. We drove to his place on the outskirts of town, and when we went inside, I was puzzled that nobody else was there. Then I realized that there wasn't going to be any party. He had lied. It was just the two of us, and his intentions now were clear.

In the moment he raped me I cried out, "GOD, WHY?!?" But there was no answer. All I saw in my mind was a black void, as though I had been catapulted into complete darkness, utterly and completely alone.

I have no idea how, in my shock, I managed to find my way back in the dark through the unfamiliar town to the B&B where I was staying, but somehow I did.

That night I had a dream.

I'm on a ship out at sea. I see my mother standing in a stairwell looking at me, wearing my scarf, the scarf I just left behind when I fled Seamus's place. She is weak, in distress. She calls out my name, but there is nothing I can do to help her. Before my eyes, she collapses and dies.

I left town as soon as I could. I took the early bus to Galway and from there traveled to Dublin, where I checked into a hotel.

When I walked into my hotel room, I set my bags down and went over to the dormer window to look out over the rooftops of Dublin. In shock and feeling desperately alone, I gazed out the window, trying to take in the reality of what had happened. Just then something on the floor caught my eye, something lying in the narrow crack between the wall and the bed, catching the light.

I bent down and picked it up. It was an Irish penny.

"He raped *you!"* Tricia said, gesturing emphatically. "You're not responsible for his actions. *He* is!"

Tricia was taking me to task. I had told our Explorations in Ministry group the story of my rape, saying it was my fault because I shouldn't have trusted a stranger. Tricia didn't say anything to contradict me at the time, but afterward, when we were alone together, she confronted me. She was completely empathetic, but she wasn't going to let me get away with the self-blame.

"He's the one who did what he did. The shame belongs to *him!"*

I knew I couldn't avoid it any longer. The time had come for me to deal with my rape, and breaking my silence was only the first step. I signed up for a training Tricia had taken at the local rape crisis center to become a counselor. The training, led by the center's director—a Presbyterian clergywoman—was tremendously empowering. We learned the shocking statistics regarding sexual violence, and how, unlike other crimes, it is usually blamed on the victim.

I also started working with a therapist, Linda, at the seminary's counseling center. Having the supportive presence of these two powerful, skillful women in my life enabled me to begin the arduous path toward healing.

I had no idea at the time that working through the trauma of my rape would prove to be only the tip of the iceberg.

It was the first semester of my second year at SFTS. I came into my dorm room and threw my book bag down on my bed. I had just come home from the noon chapel service, and I was angry.

I was fed up with all these stupid demands to use gender-inclusive language for God. The feminist students were like thought police, insisting that any masculine pronouns and imagery for God be avoided—or at least balanced with feminine pronouns and imagery.

Recently, whenever I heard someone call God "She" or "Mother" or "Sophia," I felt a fiery anger inside.

It was ridiculous that they were making such a big deal of it. *For God's sake*, I thought, *they're just pronouns!*

But then I turned the question on myself. If they were just pronouns, why was I so upset by them?

When I realized the reason for my anger, I was aghast. I was offended because calling God "She" was an affront to God—*because women are inferior!*

Stunned to see the sexism I had internalized, I suddenly recognized that unconsciously I had always refused to see myself as a woman. To be a woman was to be inferior, stupid, weak. I refused to be inferior, therefore I refused to be a woman.

During my next counseling session with Linda I reported the excruciating realization I had had.

She clapped her hands together in joy. "Another one!" she said gleefully. She had clearly seen other women seminarians come to this painful but liberating realization.

Yet even this shocking insight would prove to be only a mild tremor compared to the earthquake that would hit a few months later, this time in the form of dreams.

> *I'm in the seminary library studying. The library is a garden-level room, and there are windows along the tops of the walls, just below the ceiling. Suddenly a tremendous earthquake hits, and the building begins to shake violently. Vines planted just outside the windows begin to grow at an explosive rate, shattering the glass. They fill the room. The building is about to collapse.*
>
> *I run up the stairs, out of the building, and into a sunny courtyard where everything is completely peaceful. As I walk around the courtyard I come upon a baby with the wings of a living butterfly protruding from its mouth.*

My dream terrified me even as it promised hope. An inner upheaval had begun. This devastating "earthquake" would drive me out of the "theological library"—the collection of beliefs I had inherited about God.

But what form would this earthquake take? And what would be the nature of the new life—symbolized by the baby and butterfly—that awaited me on the other side of the catastrophe? And what of the vines that would overwhelm this old belief system? Was the symbolism pointing to the scripture verse where Jesus said, "I am the vine?"

The dream left me with so many troubling questions, but I didn't have to wait long for my answers. The cataclysm came to me the very next night, in yet another dream.

> *I'm in a room with a group of people. We are taking turns telling our life stories. Everybody else has told theirs and now it's my turn. I begin by sharing my mother's story,*

how she and her mother had to flee their hometown in Nebraska and move to Colorado to get away from my mother's violent, sexually abusive father.

An old black man sitting beside me looks me in the eye and says my next words with me, "With nothing but the shirts on their backs." The look in his eyes and the way he says the words along with me convey his solidarity. He understands the experience of oppression.

Having finished telling my mother's story it's time to tell my own, but I am suddenly overcome with a profound weariness and I simply can't go on. I stand up to leave, but as I do four people from the group get up and form a gauntlet I have to walk past in order to get to the door. As I walk past them, they begin chanting in unison, like a Greek chorus, "Who raped the fulcrum? Who raped the fulcrum?"

I want to get away from their terrifying question, but they follow me out the door. I start running as fast as I can, but they keep on chanting, "Who raped the fulcrum? Who raped the fulcrum?"

I am running so fast I become airborne. I'm flying, desperate to flee their chanting, but it pursues me.

"WHO RAPED THE FULCRUM? WHO RAPED THE FULCRUM?"

I cannot escape. Finally I scream my answer: "GOD!!!"

I woke with my heart pounding. Early in the morning I called Tricia.

"I just had a nightmare. As I was waking up from it an image flashed into my mind of a statue of Zeus as a swan, and he's raping a woman."

"Leda and the Swan."

I knew she would know. I also knew she would understand how shattering the dream was when I told it to her.

The dream was exposing God as a rapist. This male God had ordained a hierarchy of the sexes, had sanctioned the oppression of women, had set the stage for rape. Rape was part of the divine order of things.

The agony was nearly unbearable. If God—*God*—was against me, who could be for me? Where was the Court of Appeals I could turn to in order to right this injustice?

The excruciating message of the dream was clear, but what was the meaning behind the symbolism of the fulcrum? Why did the dream say it was the fulcrum that had been raped?

Then it came to me. A fulcrum is a point of strength. It gives a person the power to do things they otherwise couldn't. These were the very things the God I had been taught to believe in had stripped from me as a woman. By divinely ordaining the subjugation of women, God had violated the essence of my strength. God had raped my power.

When the dream came in January of my second year, we were in the middle of our intensive Greek course. Sitting in class, I struggled to concentrate, my heart aching unbearably as I came to grips with the message of the dream. The feeling of betrayal was beyond words.

And yet even in the midst of the pain I was enduring, I somehow knew that there was a divine Force behind the dream that was working for my wholeness, a Force that would stop at nothing to destroy the false beliefs that had so wounded and imprisoned my psyche and spirit. The misogynist god—fashioned by men—had been unmasked as a rapist and a fraud. I could worship that god no longer.

I decided to enact a ritual in response to the dream. I made a small abstract drawing depicting the God of Life, full of beautiful colors and vibrant images of new birth, including a butterfly. Attached to it was an ominous red phallus depicting the violence of misogyny and rape. When the drawing was finished I cut the phallus off and set it on fire with a candle. Dropping it into a bowl, I watched it burn, curling into ash as the delicate lines of flame danced across the paper. Just as the last speck of flame went out, the candlewick drooped over and its flame was extinguished in a pool of red wax. The rapist god was dead.

"I just don't know if I can stay in the Church," I told Tricia, weeping, as we sat together after our New Testament class.

She was crying too. "I know. I feel so betrayed. What are we going to do?"

She was going through a similar struggle. Neither of us knew if we could remain in a religious tradition that had the underpinnings of misogyny woven into its very fabric. One consolation was that we were facing it together.

I had come to seminary knowing beyond a doubt that the ministry was the right path for me. Now all of that was in question.

It was my third year of seminary. I was doing my internship at a church in Tucson, Arizona, and was about to meet with some of the men in the congregation and fill them in on what the women's group I had been leading with one of the co-pastors had been discussing.

As soon as the group of about twenty men began to assemble in the chapel I had a feeling of dread. I could feel their resistance. Some of them sat with arms defiantly crossed, others even refused to sit in the circle, pulling their chairs away. I was the only woman in the room.

I began to share with them some of the shocking statistics about violence against women in our culture. I told them about some of the experiences the women had revealed during our time together, experiences that had left them alternately angry and in tears.

That's when an older man, who had been growing increasingly agitated, burst out, "That's the problem with women these days! They think they're important! If they'd read the Bible they'd know better!"

I felt as though a knife had been plunged into my already wounded heart. And almost as painful as his words was the other men's silence. I felt certain that most of them disagreed with him, but none of them challenged his misogyny. None of them came to my defense.

It was painfully ironic that the Bible I had once revered was now being used as a weapon against me. I remembered an evening when I was in grade school: There had been torrential rains in the mountains, and the creek in our neighborhood was in danger of flooding. My parents sat in the living room, anxiously listening to the radio newscast to find out if we would have to evacuate. I thought it was thrilling, and if we were going to evacuate I wanted to be ready. So I went to my bedroom and looked around at all my childhood treasures, deciding what to take. I chose only two things: my white and tan plastic horse and my Bible. I came back to the living room with my horse and Bible in hand and told my parents, "If we have to go, I'm ready!"

Ultimately we didn't have to evacuate, but I experienced a tremendous feeling of satisfaction that night knowing that I had chosen well. After all, what else did you really need other than the Word of God and your horse?

Fortunately, my experience with the men's group was an anomaly. In all other respects my internship at First Christian Church was ideal. A progressive church near the University of Arizona campus, it was an open-minded, open-hearted congregation, and my time there convinced me that church ministry was still an option for me. It would just have to be the right church.

While in Tucson I helped lead worship services and the youth group, designed and led a workshop on inclusive language, and taught a series of classes organized through the university chaplain's office about sexual assault. I also became involved in the Sanctuary Movement, which was helping refugees from Central America, primarily El Salvador, flee the wars and political persecution in their homelands.

At one of the Sanctuary meetings we discussed how to get Juana, a Salvadoran woman whose husband had spoken out about the violence and corruption of the military in their country, across the border. The couple, along with their children, had been forced to flee to Guatemala when the death squads had come for them. But while they were in Guatemala they had gotten word that the military had come to Juana's father's house looking for them and, not finding them, had badly beaten him. Juana had gone back with the children to help her father. A month later the military had come looking for Juana's husband again—and when they didn't find him, they beat and raped her. She became pregnant, and not long after her father died from his wounds, she gave birth to a daughter, Isabel.

Now Juana and the baby, along with her two other young children, had set out to rejoin her husband, who had made it to Georgia and was awaiting them there. From there they planned to travel to Canada to seek asylum. Juana and her children had made it to the Mexican border, but so far every attempt to get them across the border had been unsuccessful. One of her children was very sick, so there was no time to waste. We needed a new plan.

A couple of days after that meeting, three of us set out early one morning for the border. We drove as far as we could, then hiked along a stream bed through the blistering heat of the desert sun. We wore drab clothing that would blend in with the landscape, taking care nonetheless to duck under cover whenever a plane approached, knowing it was likely to be the Border Patrol conducting aerial surveys.

One of the two women I was with was in her forties, the other in her seventies. The backbone of the Sanctuary Movement, I had discovered, was not made up of young radicals. Most of the volunteers were people of deep faith— many of them gray-haired women—who were courageously carrying out the acts of compassion they believed God was asking of them, even if that meant defying the laws of their government.

After a few hours of hiking we reached our rendezvous point at the border, and there, approaching from the other side, were Juana and her children, guided by two other Sanctuary volunteers.

Juana looked exhausted. She had traveled thousands of miles, caring for her young children while also managing her constant fear of being detained and deported. As soon as she saw us approaching, relief washed over her face.

In her arms she carried Isabel, bundled in a blanket. When we reached the barbed wire fence, she handed her over to me. Feeling the warmth of the baby's small body in my arms, I thought about the brutal circumstances in which she had been conceived, and tears filled my eyes.

Once Juana and her other two children had climbed through the barbed wire fence, we began our long hike back along the desert stream. Along the way, Juana had to continually remind the children, who were too young to understand the risks we were facing, to be very quiet and stay together.

When we reached a field where we could wait while one of the women retrieved the car, we nestled down in a small depression in the tall grass. We heard two men approaching on horseback, possibly Border Patrol, and we prayed that the baby wouldn't cry. Fortunately she remained quiet, and the men passed by within a few yards of us, oblivious to our presence.

We brought the family back to Tucson that day, where they rested for a while before continuing their long journey to Georgia to be reunited with Juana's husband and continue their trek to Canada, where they could receive political asylum.

I felt relieved that we had gotten Juana and her children this far, but I was worried about the dangers still ahead for her family. I knew if they were caught and deported back to El Salvador they would be killed.

Between the opportunities First Christian gave me to engage with important social justice issues and the role models I found in my two wonderful co-pastors, my internship church was the perfect setting to recover from the traumatic upheavals of the previous year—but even so, I continued to wrestle with my conflicted feelings about Jesus.

On the one hand, I wanted nothing to do with a male savior whose gender was used to reinforce the belief that God was male. On the other hand, I saw in his teachings a radical egalitarianism, and in his crucifixion I saw him suffering at the hands of the power structure just as women had for thousands of years.

Being at First Christian was a blessing, but it wasn't the only one bestowed on me that year. Another was the blossoming relationship between me and one of my seminary classmates: Kip, a gifted jazz pianist whom I had grown to love for his gentle heart, poetic sensibility, and musical soul.

For the first couple of years in seminary, Kip and I had been little more than acquaintances, but our relationship had begun to deepen shortly before I left for Tucson. He was doing his internship in Portland, sharing an apartment with Tricia and Stephen, and he and I stayed in touch by correspondence and by phone. When we returned to campus the fall of our senior year we became engaged.

My last year of seminary was devoted to completing my course requirements, taking my ordination exams, and planning our wedding, which was held two months before graduation.

As the year ended and my journey through seminary came to its conclusion, I felt as though I had gone through a crucible. What I had thought would be nothing more than an academic hoop to jump through had turned into a tumultuous and painful, but ultimately liberating and healing, experience that had completely altered the landscape of my beliefs.

All my certainties had been demolished; now I faced the daunting task of extricating the ideas about god from the living Presence that had begun to break into my life.

I didn't know anymore what I believed, or even if I belonged. But in my core I knew the demolition, painful though it was, had been necessary. Ultimately it had been a liberating gift, one that had left me with many questions. I expressed them in a poem I wrote just before graduation:

Wilderness
Four years later
and I have more questions than when I started.
My compass has become demagnetized
and it doesn't seem to matter.

Wilderness is wilderness is wilderness.
And it may be that you stumble one day
upon a river Jordan.
But it's just as likely
you'll stand on the mountaintop—
after climbing your way to the summit—
to gaze in search of milk and honey
and see nothing but haze and heat waves
rising from the desert floor.

So you may as well pause and consider
each blade of grass that grows miraculously
from the parched desert sand.

Because maybe the wilderness
is the promised land.

Chapter 7: Life in the Heartland

That's so sweet! I thought, feeling sincere affection for the menfolk as I sat in our adult Sunday School class watching a video of religious art, all of which depicted God as a bearded old man. *They made God look just like them!*

That's when I knew that the traumas of seminary were behind me. The portrayal of God as male no longer seemed threatening, nor did it kindle any anger. It just seemed amusing, endearing even.

Kip and I were now living in Missouri, co-pastoring a Presbyterian church in the small town of Butler, and somehow, over time, the chaff and the wheat had sorted themselves out. I could see Christianity's sexism for what it was: a product of humanity's patriarchal phase, not some cosmic truth. The hierarchy of the sexes was man-made. It had no bearing on what I saw as the essence of Christianity: its concern for justice, compassion, peace, and healing.

After graduation, Tricia, Stephen, Kip, and I had spent a few months in Boise living with our seminary friends Gwen and Matt, exploring the possibility of starting an intentional community together. We hadn't managed to come to a consensus about what kind of community we really wanted, though, so Stephen had accepted a call to pastor a church in San Jose, and he and Tricia moved back to California. Kip and I, meanwhile, had scrambled to find a church where we could co-pastor, and found it in Missouri.

Living in the Midwest was a new experience for us. There was a quiet simplicity to life there that appealed to me. Many people in Butler had lived in the town or surrounding farmland all their lives, and because most everybody knew most everybody else, there was a refreshing level of trust. The first time we shopped at the family-owned grocery store on the corner of the town square, the cashier told us we didn't need to pay for our groceries if we didn't want to. We could just start a tab.

When we went over to the office window to set it up with the owner, I asked, "How often do we need to pay it off?"

He shrugged. "Whenever you want to." Seeing the amazement on my face, he said, "Don't worry, we trust you," adding, with a wink, "and we know where to find you."

As co-pastors, Kip and I visited parishioners, wrote articles for the newsletter, presided at funerals, planned committee meetings, attended gatherings of the Ministerial Alliance, volunteered as chaplains in the county hospital, and took turns planning worship and preaching.

In our spare time, we did as midwesterners do. Kip put in a large vegetable garden behind the manse, winning the respect of many of the seasoned farmers with his gardening skills. I planted flowerbeds, learned how to quilt, and discovered my fondness for the prairie, with its wildflowers and songs of meadowlarks and cardinals.

Beneath the Norman Rockwell veneer, though, not all was well with the community. Small-town America had been under siege for a couple of decades, and the people had watched their way of life slowly erode. Bank foreclosures and corporate agriculture had led to the loss of farms that had been in families for generations. Small shop owners had seen their stores go belly-up when Walmart moved to town and strategically undersold them. They were caught in a devastating downward economic spiral that had taken its toll on the spirit of the people. Poverty in the region was extreme and many people couldn't afford decent homes. (This last issue prompted Kip and me to work with others in town to establish a Habitat for Humanity chapter in our county.)

The congregation also had its challenges, from mundane matters like trying to keep the sump pump in the basement working to more daunting challenges like trying to stay afloat financially with a dwindling membership. Besides the fact that churchgoing wasn't the norm it had once been, many of the younger generation had also moved away.

Although the people in our congregation were pretty tolerant and open-minded, Butler was in the Bible Belt, and every now and then I would come face-to-face with the disturbing underbelly of the religious conservatism in the area.

One day while I was working at the church alone, I heard the front door open and went to see who it was. A young woman whom I had never seen before was standing in the foyer, looking around nervously. I went over to her.

"Can I help you?"

"Is this a gay-friendly church?" she whispered, as if afraid someone else might hear her.

I answered her as best I could. "Our congregation hasn't had an open discussion about homosexuality, but they're friendly people. I think you'd be welcome here."

After she left, I never saw her again.

Another time I got a call from the hospital asking if I would come visit a patient who had requested to see me. I was puzzled. He was someone I had seen around town from time to time but I didn't know him well. He belonged to another church, and I didn't know why he wasn't asking his own pastor to visit him.

When I went to the hospital, I found out he'd been depressed and had attempted suicide. As we spoke I knew there was something he wasn't saying.

"Gary, you know you can tell me anything you need to," I finally said. "It's okay."

In a hushed voice, he came out with his crushing secret. "I'm gay. If the people at my church ever find out, they'll ostracize me. I couldn't bear that." The anguish in his voice was heartbreaking. "I've prayed and prayed to be healed."

"There's nothing to heal," I said. "God made you to be exactly who you are, and loves you just as you are." But I could tell that the self-loathing he had internalized from his religious upbringing was too extreme. He couldn't hear what I was saying.

One day after he'd been released from the hospital he came to see me in my office. During our visit it came time for him to take his meds. He took the pills out, reverently cradled them in his palm for a moment, and then with trembling hands lifted them and the glass of water to his mouth.

The words "This is my body, this is my blood" flooded my mind. I was witnessing a tragic sacrament. His church abhorred people like him, so his medications had become his surrogate communion. This was the only thing that kept him from falling into the dark abyss of despair and self-destruction. I was outraged and distressed that a religion that claimed to follow the teachings of Jesus—who welcomed and loved outcasts—had become such a judgmental and destructive force that it could drive someone to try to take his own life. I shuddered to remember that there was a time in my life when I had harbored such intolerant beliefs.

One morning I was going through the church mail and came upon a newsletter that said the Presbyterian Church needed volunteers to go to Guatemala to accompany a Mayan woman who was receiving death threats. The woman's husband, a Mayan Presbyterian pastor named Manuel, had been abducted and tortured by the military, apparently because of his human rights work. His mutilated body had been discovered buried in a cornfield outside the military compound.

When Manuel's widow, María, also began receiving death threats, she and her children fled their hometown for Guatemala City. The Presbyterian Church in the US and Canada was arranging for people to stay with them to make it clear that the international community was watching. I volunteered, and within a few weeks was on my way to Guatemala.

I was with María on a bus, returning to Guatemala City from the market in Antigua, when we came to an unexpected halt. The driver shut off the engine and the Latin music coming from the loudspeakers went dead.

"If they come for me, tell them you don't know me," María whispered to me.

The door swung open. A soldier boarded.

The passengers fell silent. Cradling his machine gun, the soldier slowly surveyed the crowd. Shadowed by the visor of his military cap, his face was like stone: hard, expressionless.

I could feel María's fear. Her leg was bouncing up and down next to mine as she tried to mask her panic with an expression of nonchalance.

Her instruction to pretend I didn't know her made no sense to me. After all, the reason I was there accompanying her was so that the military would know that people from North America were with her. But I didn't have time to ask for an explanation.

In the previous year she had done all she could to change her appearance. She had cut her long, black braid, abandoned her Mayan dress for western clothing—wearing blue jeans and a white blouse instead of the colorful embroidered huipil of her ancestors. But still she was afraid the military might recognize her. Her ID card had recently been misplaced or stolen, and she feared they now had her photo with her updated appearance.

I studied the soldier's face. He was so young. What had he been like before the army had shaped him?

I tried to strike a balance in my demeanor, neither avoiding eye contact, which might arouse suspicion, nor focusing my gaze too intently on him, which might also draw his attention.

After an eternal moment, he turned, got off the bus, and waved us on.

On the surface, things looked so normal. People were going about their business, doing their daily activities. But some of María's acquaintances would speak to her in hushed voices about what was really going on. One day one of her friends in the marketplace told her about the torture he had endured while held prisoner by the military.

"They used *la capucha* on me," he whispered, referring to the rubber hood placed over a person's head to create the panic of suffocation.

One day María and I left the house early to catch the bus down to a remote location on the coast where a friend of hers lived. When we arrived, Rosa served us breakfast on her front porch—homemade corn tortillas, fried plantain, and black beans. While we ate, the two women talked about Rosa's neighbors half a mile down the road.

"One night," Rosa said, "when the older children were home from college, the military came. They broke down the door and gunned down the family. One of the youngest children fled out the back of the house, out into the field, but they gunned her down as she ran." She continued, her voice full of emotion, "A woman I know asked a soldier once why they killed the children. He said it was because they didn't want them to grow up learning hatred."

I was dumbstruck. "When did this happen?" I asked.

Rosa's voice dropped so low I couldn't hear her, and I asked her to repeat what she had said. "Rios Montt," she whispered again, telling me not when but *who*.

Rios Montt had been the military dictator of Guatemala in the early '80s. His regime, which had received financial support from the US government, had been notorious for massacres, tortures, rapes, and genocide against the indigenous population. He summarized his political philosophy in a single maxim: "Beans for the obedient. Bullets for the rest." Montt, a military general, was also an evangelical pastor.

I was floored that even now, thirteen years later, Rosa still could only speak his name in a whisper.

One night, staying with María, I had a dream. In the dream I was in a worship service in which we were singing a beautiful, moving hymn that began with the words "*De la paz.*" Of peace. I woke with the melody still floating in my head, though most of the lyrics had faded, leaving behind only the feeling they had imparted. I got up and wrote the melody down, and when I returned home did my best to recreate the message of the lyrics.

De la paz, of peace I sing this song
For that day when war shall cease to be

When the hungry child can have her daily bread
And the one in chains has been set free.

Now the swords are hard and plowshares few
And the wolf still preys upon the lamb
But in far-off hills there sounds a rolling stream
Of the justice promised by I Am.

Yet this path we walk is long and steep
And we're tired and have so far to go
But our weary feet can still take one more step
And our hands one seed of peace can sow.

With each step that time of peace draws near
Even though it may not dawn today
For we know through humble acts of our short lives
God's love will somehow work its way.

De la paz, of peace I dream this dream
That shalom will one day live in me
When the blindness in my soul at last is healed
And in captives' eyes the Christ I'll see. I'll see.

The following year I was sent by the Presbyterian denomination to Honduras to participate in a conference of fifty pastors and theologians from the US and fifty from Latin America. We discussed the newest form of imperialism—neo-liberal globalization—which was threatening the working class in the US and impoverishing countless people in Latin America. Under the pretense of "free trade," it was resulting in a dramatic flow of wealth from the poorest and most vulnerable to the richest and most powerful.

I felt passionately that these issues were central to the Christian faith. Jesus, who lived under imperial Rome, had stood in solidarity with the poor and marginalized. Like María's husband Manuel, Jesus had been tortured and executed as an enemy of the state.

We had been in Butler for four years now, and it was becoming clear that it was time for us to move on. While I cherished the people of our congregation and their beautiful practice of caring for one another, the quiet simplicity of small-town living that at first had seemed so novel had begun to feel stifling to me. I believed strongly that the Church was meant to be the body of Christ, advocating for the oppressed and marginalized. I needed to find a congregation that shared my passion for social justice. I knew, though, that such churches were few and far between.

Our time in Butler had persuaded Kip that parish ministry wasn't a good fit for him. He said he was willing to follow me wherever my path led. So I wrote a candid dossier, clearly expressing my beliefs and describing the kind of congregation I wanted to serve, and decided to give my search two years. If after that time I still hadn't found a good match, I would do something different with my life.

Chapter 8: Beloved Community

"But here's the question," I said to the children. "If Jesus rose from the dead, then *where is he?*"

I looked around Tabernacle's packed sanctuary as birdsong and sunlight poured in on a gorgeous Easter morning in Philadelphia.

"Where *is* the body of Christ?" I asked again, a puzzled look on my face.

In a matter of seconds the congregation was on its feet. I was nearly in tears.

It had taken only five months for me to receive a call to a congregation that was a dream come true.

I had looked mostly at churches in the West and Southwest, but there was one church in Philadelphia that had intrigued me. Tabernacle United Church, or Tab as its congregation members called it, described itself as a small, progressive, urban church looking for a theologically and socially progressive pastor. They were a union church belonging to two denominations—Presbyterian and United Church of Christ—and they had been the first congregation in Pennsylvania of either denomination to openly include LGBT people in full membership and leadership. They used inclusive language in their worship services, had been a Sanctuary church during the wars in Central America, and continued to maintain a relationship with a village in El Salvador. Over the years they had launched several nonprofits that worked on social justice concerns. The match couldn't have been more perfect.

Kip and I moved to Philadelphia shortly before Thanksgiving 1997, into an apartment a short walking distance from the church. Each morning, walking the red brick sidewalk on my way to work, I marveled at the turn my life had taken.

Tabernacle's beautiful neo-Gothic building stood adjacent to the University of Pennsylvania's campus, but the real treasure was the people. They had an authenticity and spiritual depth that I had never before encountered in a congregation. In worship they prayed with an unpretentious candor and laughed at irreverent humor, and during the time of joys and concerns they shared openly and honestly. It was clear they didn't come to church because they felt a social obligation to be there. They were there because they wanted to express and explore their spiritual lives together.

Even though I had never bought into Calvin's notorious belief in predestination, by every measure it seemed like I was supposed to be there—and that feeling only deepened as I started to notice more and more odd connections between Tabernacle and myself.

During my search for a new church, when I first became interested in Tab, Kip suggested I call Tricia's husband, Stephen. Kip remembered that Stephen had once lived in Philadelphia and thought he might know something about Tab, so I called him up.

"Kip tells me you used to live in Philadelphia."

"I did."

"He suggested I call you because I've been sending my dossier out and there's a church in Philadelphia I'm interested in."

"What church is it?"

"Tabernacle."

"My dad used to be the pastor at Tab."

"Are you kidding me?"

"No. And you remember Laurie from seminary? Her father was also a pastor at Tab."

"No way! I know him. He was a Presbytery colleague of ours. In fact, he gave us his *Interpreter's Bible* after he retired and he and his wife were moving." The encyclopedic set of scholarly research and commentary on the scriptures had become a cherished resource for me.

Another odd coincidence happened the day before I flew to Philadelphia for my interview with Tab's pastoral search committee. Kip and I had flown to Atlanta for his sister's wedding, which I was to sing for. Kip was accompanying me on the piano, and the day before the wedding, while we were rehearsing in the sanctuary, a man wandered in and sat down in one of the pews. After we finished I went over and greeted him.

"Hi," I said, reaching out to shake his hand.

"Hello. I hope you don't mind me stopping in to listen. My daughter's a musician who often sings at weddings. What song were you singing?"

"It's one I wrote for my sister-in-law's wedding tomorrow."

"Could I get a copy of it? I'd love to give it to her."

I smiled, flattered. "I wish I could give you one, but I don't have it written out. My husband, Kip, is accompanying me and he's just working off a chord chart. What brought you here?"

"I'm here for a meeting. I'm a United Church of Christ pastor."

"Oh!" I exclaimed, delighted. "I'm leaving right after the wedding tomorrow to fly to Philadelphia to interview with a pastoral search committee. It's a union church—Presbyterian and UCC."

"Oh, Tab?" he said.

I was floored that this stranger, who had just happened to wander into the sanctuary while we were rehearsing, knew about the church almost eight hundred miles away that I had my heart set on.

After Kip and I moved to Philadelphia I started to read about Tab's history. I found out that one of their first pastors, William Henry Oxtoby, had left Tabernacle in 1913 to take up a teaching position at San Francisco Theological Seminary and later became the seminary's president. All through seminary I had lived in the dorm that was named after him.

I also found out that one of the Sanctuary volunteers who had helped us get Juana across the border had also been involved with Tab.

These and other strange connections made Tabernacle feel even more like the place where I belonged. I had never been happier, despite some sorrows.

My father died unexpectedly in January 1999. He had suffered a stroke, and though he survived, it had left him unable to speak or write. The doctor didn't think he was in any danger of dying, so Mom told my brothers and me that there wasn't any need for us to come right away. Because he couldn't speak, I didn't try calling him, either.

I wish I had. One morning when my mother came to visit him in the hospital, she found him dead.

I had known that the hardest thing about moving to Philadelphia would be living so far from my parents, who were in their late seventies by this point. Even though they wanted me to go where I felt called, it weighed on me that

I wouldn't be closer to help them in their old age or accompany them in their dying.

Kip and I flew to Denver for Dad's memorial service, and while I was there I took a walk along the creek near my parents' house. The morning was brisk and clear, the sky a deep blue, and the snow-capped Rockies to the west shone in the sunlight.

I watched a pair of mallard ducks paddling in the creek, their wakes intermingling. Suddenly I was pierced with the terrifying realization of the impermanence of things, the naked truth of mortality. My father, who had been a presence all of my life, was gone, and I had had no chance to say good-bye.

Three months after my father's death, I was sitting in my office at the church one day when I got a phone call from Kip.

"You might want to turn on the news," he said, his voice somber. "There's a terrible shooting going on in Colorado."

"Where?"

"Columbine."

Columbine? I racked my brain trying to think where Columbine, Colorado was. Maybe a little town in the mountains? Or on the prairie? I simply couldn't place a town with that name.

"Columbine, Colorado?"

"Columbine High School."

I was shocked. I knew exactly where Columbine High School was. After coming back from the Peace Corps, my first teaching assignment had been at Columbine. I could picture the hallways, the classrooms, the library, the parking lot. That such an ordinary suburban school just a few miles from where I grew up could become the scene of a nightmare was beyond belief.

I called my mother that evening. She and some friends had been at a shopping mall just a couple miles from the school when it happened.

"There were so many police helicopters circling overhead and emergency vehicles racing down Wadsworth that we knew something was happening. Now the Red Cross is asking people to go to the blood banks."

Over the course of the following days, every morning when I left for work I was greeted by two starkly contrasting realities: the blossoming beauty of Philadelphia's springtime, and the newspaper lying on the porch with its huge headlines and photographs reporting the unfolding details of an atrocity that had happened in a familiar place thousands of miles away.

By now Kip had taken a job in his previous field of technology, and we were both enjoying living in Philadelphia. Center City was a vibrant hub of culture, with world-class art museums, theaters, and music. Old City was a treasure trove of history with narrow cobblestone streets, red brick colonial houses, Independence Hall, and the Liberty Bell.

I also felt an affinity with the vision of William Penn—founder of the city—a Quaker committed to religious tolerance, nonviolence, and peaceful relations with the native inhabitants of the land.

Philadelphia's park system, one of the largest in the country, was yet another treasure. Meandering along the Schuylkill River and Wissahickon Creek, it encompassed vast open spaces as well as large swaths of woods. All I had to do was drive a few miles from home to find myself in the midst of nature.

But the city had many challenges. I was shocked when I first rode through the "bombed out" areas of the city. Neighborhoods that had once been thriving hubs of activity during Philadelphia's industrial heyday now looked like ghost towns. For miles on end, abandoned factory build-ings—windows broken out, brick walls covered with graffiti, lots overgrown with weeds—sprawled over the landscape. The poverty in the forsaken neighborhoods, mostly African American, was shocking. Violence, much of it drug-related, was epidemic.

The economic disparity rivaled what I had witnessed in Ecuador. I was appalled that such conditions existed in the United States.

One day Susan, who was a member of Tab and a good friend of mine, came to our apartment on fire with an idea.

"Oh my gosh!" she said as soon as I opened the door. "I've got to tell you about this idea I've had! You know that bookstore I told you about that was going out of business? Well I went there a couple days ago and a book literally jumped off the shelf at me. So I bought it. It's by a woman who's an artist-in-residence at a retreat center, and I was so inspired! And I realized that's what I want to do!! Not be an artist-in-residence, exactly. But I want to help people tap into their creativity!"

Susan was a gifted painter and knew from personal experience the healing power of art-making. Creativity had become central in my own spiritual life as well. Whenever I was writing music I felt like I was tapping into something much bigger than myself. So I was completely on board with her idea.

"Maybe we could start something at Tab," I said. "There are lots of people in the congregation who are into the arts. Combining creativity with healing would be a perfect fit! I'll bring it up with the church council at our next meeting."

A couple days later, while I was in my office writing a letter to our council about Susan's idea, I was thinking about people unleashing the power of their imaginations and creativity— something which, I had a strong feeling, was essential not only for our individual well-being but for our collective future. As I composed the letter every cell in my being was vibrating, "YES!"

Suddenly I noticed a stream of dark liquid inching its way across my desk. My can of Tab soda had sprung a leak.

The can of Tab had been a prop for a skit I had written for the church's 125th anniversary two years earlier. I had kept it on my desk ever since, as a symbol of the eerie connections and deep bond I felt with the congregation.

I picked up the can and looked for the leak but couldn't see anything. Mystified, I put the can in a bowl and kept writing. After I finished the letter, I noticed that the can had stopped leaking, so I wiped it off and set it back on my desk, where it sat without spilling another drop.

That month the council voted to launch what we dubbed the Arts and Spirituality Center. Over the next several years, under Susan's leadership, the Center grew into ArtWell, a thriving nonprofit working with tens of thousands of youth across the city, mostly in underserved neighborhoods. Bringing a glimmer of light to some of the city's most forsaken neighborhoods, ArtWell helped young people discover their creative gifts, claim possibilities for their lives, develop their skills as leaders, and envision their communities at peace.

The week after the council voted to launch this new ministry, Kip and I flew out to California to spend a couple of weeks with Tricia and Stephen. Tricia and I went out to lunch one day and she talked with me about the possibility of getting a bone marrow transplant.

She had been diagnosed with aplastic anemia before we ever met—her immune system was attacking the red blood cells as they formed in her bone marrow. Over the years she had become increasingly dependent on blood transfusions.

Now her body was reaching the limit of its tolerance for transfusions, so she was faced with a choice: let the disease run its course until she died, or undergo the transplant.

Sitting across from me in the restaurant booth, she talked about the decision she faced.

"Every time I think about a transplant, it feels like entering the dragon's mouth."

How like her, I thought, to come up with such a mythical metaphor. I was happy to play along. "Maybe you could create a mythic story about entering the dragon's mouth and coming out victorious," I suggested.

Her face lit up. "That's a great idea!" She fell silent for a moment as she thought it over. "It actually feels like it's time for me to have a new myth. All my life it's been 'The Elephant's Child'."

When she had told me, years earlier, that her favorite story was Rudyard Kipling's "The Elephant's Child," she'd voiced surprise that I had never heard the tale—how the Elephant's Child, driven by its "'satiable curtiosity," ended up in a life-or-death tugging match with the Crocodile on "the banks of the great grey-green greasy Limpopo River," where the Elephant's stubby nose got stretched into a very useful trunk.

Tricia liked the story because she had been equally unrelenting in her search for answers. Like the Elephant's Child, her curiosity had not always been welcome, but the quest had always changed her for the better.

One of the questions she had long sought to answer was what had caused her disease. She never knew for sure, but she always suspected it might have stemmed from the summer outings she and her family took when she was a child, when they went swimming in the Columbia River. They were unaware at the time—because the public wasn't informed until years later—that upstream, at the Hanford Site, radioactive waste was being dumped into the river.

Chapter 9: Entering the Dragon's Mouth

I stood in the doorway of Tricia's hospital room, shocked. If it hadn't been for the unmistakable Cheshire Cat grin that lit up her face when she saw me, I might not have recognized her. With her bald head and swollen face, she looked more like the Buddha than Tricia.

After first going to the sink to wash my hands—part of the rigorous transplant wing protocol—I went over to her bed.

"Can I hug you?" I asked.

"Of course!"

I was gentle, not wanting to disturb the Hickman line that was sticking out of her chest.

It had been just a few weeks after our visit together in the summer that Tricia had called me saying they had found a bone marrow donor and she had decided to go forward with the transplant in Seattle. She had asked me to come out to be her first caregiver after the procedure. I had asked our church council for the time off, and they had sent me with their blessings.

Despite the jarring transformation in Tricia's appearance, I was overjoyed to see her. Soon we were cracking jokes and laughing so loudly that people down the hall could hear us.

After the initial exuberance of my arrival had worn off, however, Tricia became withdrawn. She had to devote what little energy she had to her fight to stay alive. I had brought my guitar, and sometimes I would sing for her or read aloud to her, but most of the time she simply rested while I attended the hospital's classes for caregivers.

Living on the other side of the country, I hadn't witnessed the agonizing details of my friend's slow decline, but one afternoon I got a glimmer of what she had been through.

Two nurses came to Tricia's room to pull out her Hickman line, which had become infected.

"Could you step out into the hallway for a moment?" one of them said to me.

I left the room and closed the door behind me. Soon I heard Tricia scream with pain.

When the nurses opened the door, with blood and pus spattered on their scrubs and goggles, one of them said, "You might want to go in and hold her hand."

I sat down in the chair next to her bed and took her hand in mine. I could feel her deep exhaustion.

"Maybe you can get an idea of what it's been like for me," she said quietly.

Tears rose in my eyes. I nodded, not knowing what to say.

She closed her eyes and was quiet for a moment. "I saw a movie once," she finally said, her eyes still closed as though she were seeing the scenes in her mind. "It took place in Scotland several centuries ago. It was about some villagers whose homes had been plundered and burned—and the women raped—by marauding bands. Despite it all, one of the women who had been raped and whose home had been destroyed said, 'It is yet bearable.'" She opened her eyes and looked over at me. "If that woman could see her situation as 'yet bearable,' then so can I."

She was quiet again. I remained silent, knowing there was more coming.

"When it gets really bad I remember something I learned from Buddhism—that everything changes," she said. "It's the one thing I've been able to hold on to. I know no matter how bad things get, they will always change. That has brought me a lot of comfort."

One day we were taking one of our slow walks down the hallway so Tricia could build up her strength. Steadying herself with the rolling IV stand, she was telling me about her near-death experience after her reaction to one of the substances they had injected her with in preparation for the transplant.

"I was in my bed, sailing through a series of white rooms that opened up into a chamber of light. It was so peaceful and filled with well-being that I knew whatever happened to me, I would be all right. After that, I wasn't afraid anymore."

As she finished telling the story, we stopped in front of a large plate glass window at the end of the hallway to look out at the autumn landscape.

I turned to look at her as she gazed out the window. Her countenance was peaceful, but she looked so old for someone who was only in her mid-forties.

As I looked at Tricia in the soft glow of light, I suddenly knew she was going to die. The knowledge came with a calm, dispassionate clarity, as though the light coming through the window were simply delivering information.

I was deeply shaken, but managed to conceal it. In silence I walked with her back to her room, carrying with me the knowledge of a future I didn't want to see.

Early each morning Tricia and I would anxiously await the doctor's morning rounds to find out whether the lab tests showed any indication that the new bone marrow had engrafted. Day after day the news was discouraging, and I could sense Tricia struggling to hold on to hope.

But one morning the doctor came into the room elated, announcing that her neutrophil count had skyrocketed. The new bone marrow had taken hold and was doing its job. The medical staff hailed her comeback, after they had nearly lost her, as something of a miracle.

Buoyant that the new bone marrow had finally engrafted, Tricia set her sights on regaining her strength so she could begin her outpatient treatment.

As my ten days as her caregiver ended things were looking hopeful, and she and I had even started making plans to go on retreat together once she was fully recovered.

When she was finally able to return home three months later to continue her care under her doctor at Stanford, we were all overjoyed. Tricia had walked through the dragon's mouth and come out victorious. I put my troubling premonition behind me.

Then one day in early February, just days after Tricia had returned home, the phone rang.

"Hello?"

"Patrish. It's Gwen." Her voice was trembling. "Tricia's brain is bleeding and the doctors can't do anything to stop it."

Chapter 10: Rigpa

I *have had dreams about dying in the last few years.*
And I have had visions: One night because of a cold
I had trouble breathing, and a black angel sat with me
until morning, guarding me. When I woke I heard his
long, feathered wings swish along the carpet as he walked
down the hall and through the window. And I also saw
myself arriving after an exhausting journey through snow
and storm at Arienrhod's spiral castle at the back of the
north wind. There I was bathed and warmed by the
keepers and led to the Goddess of Loving Compassion.
She welcomed me into her arms and I entered, merging
with the light.

   Like all people with chronic illness or those who are
aging, my life is marked by loss. Because of my anemia I
have had to learn to let go of my drive, my compulsion to
compete, my desire to accomplish and be recognized, my
need to finish my novel, even my cherished ability to think
clearly, analyze, and articulate. Especially I have had
to let go of the desire to control my disease. Many times

I tried to change my lifestyle or seek alternate forms of health care, and believed that I could arrest the process of decline. Perhaps these all had the effect of giving me more time, for which I am grateful, but in the end the descent was inexorable.

I have few regrets. I feel that I've lived a full and productive life. I wish I hadn't wasted so much time running away from intimacy with myself and others. I wish I had understood earlier that relationships are more valuable than recognition, and that imagination is more important than knowledge. I also wish I had learned earlier to be kind to myself, to accept my own dark, underworld twin, to listen to her and to embrace her even when she offended my above-world self.

Having a life-threatening disease gave me a sense of urgency. It also pushed me to take emotional risks and to explore my inner world, which led me into psychotherapy and eventually seminary, two of the best choices of my life.

Always I was looking for the meaning of life, for Truth, for myself, and trying to find my way through the Great Doubt, my pit of despair. While I wouldn't have chosen chronic illness as the medium for my growth, looking back I can say that it forced me to change in ways I am glad for: it increased my patience, my tolerance, and my openness to different ways of being in the world.

I never found Truth, but I found some of my own truth when I changed the focus of my search for meaning from outside to inside. I finally understood that I could not fathom it all, that there is no way for the conscious mind to comprehend the universe. At one time I actually thought I could do it. What a relief to finally be able to let that go. Because I felt insecure, I wanted something solid to stand on, but I discovered that all I could count on is change. The more I sit with that the better it feels.

Now I believe that the best I can do is to become aware of and enjoy the miracle of life that is unfolding all around me, and to enjoy the miracle of my own consciousness.

I'm incredibly grateful for the love I've shared with my husband, my family, and my friends. I'm also thankful for all the people who have accompanied me on my spiritual journey.

When I could not find God in the words of the great religions, I could always find Her in nature. In the end, experiencing and trying to harmonize with the natural world, its seasons and ever-changing cycles, has given me a pattern of interrelatedness and a meaningful place in the universe. I believe in a transcendent spirit, the Great Mystery of the Universe, and that I shall meet Her face to face after I die. I anticipate that meeting with peace and joy.

I finished reading the personal statement Tricia had written to be read at her memorial service and sat back down in the pew. The morning was gray and drizzly. During the service I watched the raindrops streaking the tall window in the front of the sanctuary that looked out onto the towering trunk of a redwood tree.

When the service was over and people were heading for the fellowship room, I noticed that the light outside had changed. I went to the front door of the church and stepped outside. The sun was breaking through the clouds. A rainbow arced across the sky.

In the stunned days following Tricia's death I felt a strange euphoria. I seemed to have no barrier between myself and the natural world. The gnarled branches of an old oak, the shafts of sunlight streaming through the clouds, raindrops clinging to a spider web, the carpet of moss on a stone, all left me beside myself with amazement.

I still couldn't imagine living without my soul friend who had intuitively understood me, but initially Tricia's death evoked in me more gratitude than grief. It also awakened in me a firm resolve not to live my own life on the surface anymore. Although I had had many meaningful experiences in my life, I sensed there was something deeper to be discovered, something about the essence of my existence that had remained hidden. The time had come to find out what it was.

The morning after her service, while sitting in the stillness of Tricia's study surrounded by her altar, books, and journals, I asked her to be my Bodhisattva, guide to the awakening of my heart. I sensed she heard me.

When I returned home, I began to read her copy of *The Tibetan Book of Living and Dying*, which I had brought with me. In the margins she had penciled her comments and cryptic summaries of the book's contents, giving me a window into the depth of her spiritual explorations, what she had come to understand about life, and how she had prepared herself for death:

> "uncover our strong, fundamental goodness"
> "emptiness = no separate existence"
> "letting go is path to freedom"
> "our true nature is perfect awareness"
> "forgiveness is purifying and prepares one for death"
> "our thoughts determine direction to enlightenment or suffering"
> "rigpa = pure awareness"

I tried to absorb it all, though I knew I was only scratching the surface of the wisdom.

At the same time I felt an intense desire to learn more about quantum physics, an interest of mine which I hadn't explored in depth. It seemed like an odd longing in response to loss, yet I sensed it would point me to truths that were hidden beneath the visible surface of things.

Much of what I read seemed impossible: two particles that had once been united but then separated from each other would *simultaneously* change their spin, regardless of the distance between them. Electrons instantly jumped from one energy state to another without traversing the intervening space. Particles spontaneously appeared out of the quantum void and then vanished again just as suddenly. An electron existed in multiple places and only collapsed into a specific location when it was observed.

All of this was unfathomable. How could spatial separation be irrelevant? How could all possibilities simultaneously coexist before observation? How could matter spontaneously appear out of nothing? How could something jump from one place to another without traveling through the space between? Clearly, things were not as they seemed.

By now the finality of Tricia's death had settled upon me, and my initial euphoria had faded. The remainder of my own life stretched out before me like an empty epilogue.

What I longed for more than anything else was to go to New Mexico, to be alone in the desert and let myself sink into my grief. But I had responsibilities in Philadelphia that made that impossible. Instead I sought solace in the woods a few miles from our house, going there on pilgrimage every Friday.

It was wintertime when Tricia died, and nature, in her season of barrenness, seemed to be accompanying me in my grief. But then Good Friday came, and with it the first signs of spring.

Approaching the woods that day I saw that spindly

branches of forsythias had erupted into garments of yellow, and daffodils, having pushed their way up through the carpet of dead leaves, had flung their bodies wide in a jubilant welcome of spring.

I felt betrayed and utterly bereft. Nature was taunting me, abandoning me, moving on with her season of new beginnings, leaving me to deal with my grief alone.

My heart was raw, broken open like a shattered vessel. Never before had I felt so empty.

Aching inwardly, I followed the trail through the woods. When I came to a rise and looked out at the bare trees before me, I heard Tricia's voice say to me, "This is rigpa."

Instantly, time dropped away. The trees were no longer trees. They had become portals revealing a *presence*. Here there was no past, present, or future. Everything that ever had, ever would, or ever could exist was here. Now.

The shimmering Reality I was beholding was so vast, so intricate, so utterly devoid of judgment, so *loving* that I broke down weeping. Its beauty overwhelmed me.

Chapter 11: Elephants and Ashes

When I was in the Peace Corps, a team of eye doctors from the US once came to our village to offer a free clinic for a week, doing basic eye surgeries and dispensing hundreds of pairs of donated eyeglasses. Quichua flocked in from all over the region, many of them walking days to get there, to camp out in line and wait their turn.

Among them was a young mother with her little daughter in tow. The woman's eyesight was so poor she was essentially blind. When the medical team determined the amount of correction she required, they knew there was no way they would have a pair of glasses strong enough to come even close to what she needed. They sent her down to the chapel anyway, where the glasses were being distributed, in hopes there might be a pair strong enough to at least help her make out general shapes.

When she got to the chapel the volunteers checked the list—and they were astounded to discover that there was a pair of glasses with precisely the prescription the woman needed. When they gave them to her, for the first time in her life she was able to see her daughter. Weeping, all she could say, over and over again, was, "She's so beautiful! She's so beautiful!"

After that Good Friday in the woods when I first saw the beauty of Reality, I would never again be able to believe that death, time, or condemnation existed in any ultimate sense. Even so, I still ached with grief that Tricia was gone from this tangible plane.

Following her death, a strange thing started happening. I started noticing synchronicities involving elephants, reminding me of Tricia's favorite childhood story.

Elephants started showing up in my dreams, but also in my waking life. Once, sitting in the airport, I noticed a woman sitting directly across from me wearing a large jeweled elephant pin on her lapel. Another time I was walking down the street past a bookstore. When I glanced in the window there was an elephant staring back at me from the cover of a book prominently on display. In another instance a friend was in a shop looking for a card for me and noticed one all by itself on a table with stacks of books. It had a photo of an elephant on the front. She took it over to the cashier, who had no idea where it had come from and gave it to my friend free of charge.

When the synchronicities first started happening I felt as though I had entered some sort of twilight zone. Had elephants always been present in this way but I had never noticed them? Some of these instances just seemed too unlikely to be pure chance.

I was feeling disquieted by it all. Was Tricia trying to communicate with me? Or was I being encouraged to go in search of the answers to my deepest questions, like the Elephant's Child in Kipling's story? Would my questions about the nature of death and life lead me to tangle with a crocodile and permanently reshape my spiritual nose?

Five months after Tricia's death, Kip and I returned to California to join her friends and family in scattering her ashes in a canyon she had loved. The night before the ritual, Stephen, Gwen, Kip, and I went out to dinner to plan the event. The woman waiting our table, I noticed, was wearing a necklace with an elephant on it.

The next day—Tricia's birthday—we all gathered at the trailhead and silently hiked into the canyon, Stephen in the lead carrying Tricia's ashes. When we reached the waterfall at the trail's end, we had a simple ritual. One by one, we stepped forward to take a handful of ash.

I went off to a secluded, cool crevasse to be alone. Holding the ashes in my clenched hands, I was incredulous that this was all that was left of Tricia's body.

I remembered her laughter and her mischievous grin. I remembered our conversations in the coffee shop during seminary exploring our dreams. I remembered that long hug we'd shared last summer, before her transplant, as I was about to fly home. I remembered cradling her in my arms, singing a song for her the night before she died.

Finally, reluctantly, I insisted my clenched fists open, and through my tears watched her ashes drift to the ground.

Chapter 12: Ground Zero

Looking over the stacks of boxes the movers had left in our dining room, I couldn't believe how much stuff Kip and I had accumulated.

After months of searching, we had finally managed to buy a place. It was a fixer-upper, not at all what we had hoped for—a shabby little three-bedroom row house with an atrocious paint job on the edge of a slightly dicey neighborhood.

The morning after our moving day—two months after coming back from the ash scattering—I left the chaos of our new home behind to go to work. It was a beautiful September morning.

I listened to the radio on the drive to the church. There was a newscast in progress. They were saying something about an attack in New York City. Something about the World Trade Center. Something about airplanes and explosions, and people jumping to their deaths to escape the inferno.

When I got to the church, I parked my car and hurried down to a sports bar a block away, where dozens of televisions were displaying the same unbelievable images of chaos in the streets of New York, of flames and smoke billowing out of the twin skyscrapers, and then the utterly implausible collapse of first one, then the other tower.

I had planned to spend the afternoon of September 11th taking a few remaining belongings over to our new house, but instead I spent the day scrambling to prepare a prayer service for that evening.

At sundown we gathered in Tab's sanctuary to pray and to cry, and most of all to find solace in one another's company. We were all in shock, grief-stricken and wondering what would happen next.

That Sunday I did my best to speak about the horror. I gave a sermon based on the Lord's Prayer, which I titled "Deliver Us from Evil":

> We have all been stunned by the sights and sounds that have been seared into our memories this week, and we have probably all lived through these last days in disbelief. We know that what we have witnessed will prove to be a turning point in our nation's and the world's history, because the dust and debris from the World Trade Center has fallen not just over Lower Manhattan; its residue has descended like an ominous cloud over the whole world and has left us with a haunting question about where the human family goes from here.
>
> Tuesday saw the collapse of so much more than the two towers on the New York skyline. Tuesday brought the collapse of the hopes, the dreams, and the futures of thousands of families. Their lives as they knew them have collapsed and the ripples from their loss are spreading across the country as we begin to learn of people we know who have been affected. Our nation's isolation from the violence and suffering of the rest of the world collapsed, as well as our sense of safety and invulnerability as Ameri-

cans. *Our faith in our government's ability to detect and prevent terrorism collapsed. And, although we aren't ready to acknowledge it yet, the power of our military strength collapsed. All it took to bring down the World Trade Towers and set the Pentagon on fire, taking thousands of lives in the process, were knives and box cutters. Tuesday's events revealed in an apocalyptic way that all of our guided missiles, all of our stealth bombers, all of our aircraft carriers, all of our plans for missile defense systems will not in the end protect us from the wrath of those who see us as their enemies.*

Evil. That is a word that has been uttered frequently these last days, and understandably so. How else does one speak of what we have seen: passenger airplanes used as missiles to strike at a time of day when the act would claim the most possible casualties? How else but as evil does one describe the actions that have caused unimaginable anguish and loss to the families and friends of those who just happened to be leaving a subway station, or at their desk, or on a plane at the wrong time?

The president has said in the aftermath of Tuesday's devastation that we are now in a struggle between good and evil, and I agree. But what I fear, even more than the terrorism that struck and could strike again, is that the words "good" and "evil" are becoming in people's minds synonymous for "us" and "them." I think we all know where that thinking can lead us, and it is a frightening prospect.

Every week we pray to God to lead us not into temptation but deliver us from evil. That prayer is needed now more than ever, because now that we have experienced the horror of September 11th, we face the greatest of temptations—namely, to allow the seeds of anger and violence and hatred that were sown this week to find fertile soil and sprout and send forth roots into our own hearts.

Many years ago, when I was on a faith and resistance retreat during the arms race, there was a nun who had been a longtime nonviolent activist, and she warned us that the greatest danger in confronting evil is that it brings out the evil in us. This is the gravest danger each of us and our entire country now faces.

So let us ask ourselves, what made Tuesday's acts evil in our eyes? Was it not the calculated disregard for human life? Was it not the blind hatred expressed toward an entire population? Was it not the use of massacre and destruction to serve a political end? Was it not the religious zealotry, the belief that these acts of murder were the will of God?

If these were the things that made Tuesday's acts evil, then these are precisely the things that we as a people will be most tempted to do in return. We will be tempted to disregard human life. We will be tempted to hate an entire population. We will be tempted to massacre and destroy for our political ends, and in it all we will be tempted to believe that we are God's agents carrying out the will of the Almighty. This is the evil we must pray fervently to be delivered from. If we succumb to these temptations, then Tuesday's terrorist act will have succeeded. It will have ripped apart far more than steel and glass and the lives of five thousand people and their families. It will have ripped through the soul of our nation.

The president said at the National Cathedral on Friday that in our war on terrorism we will rid the world of evil. This is something that is beyond our ability as human beings. We cannot rid the world of evil, but we can try with every fiber of our being to rid our actions of evil. To believe that we can rid the world of evil is to set the stage for launching our own jihad, our own holy war, and then it will indeed happen, as theologian Walter Wink has said, that we become what we hate.

Let us on this day collectively mourn the lives that have been lost and the unimaginable suffering this is causing to so many thousands of people today. And let us also mourn the hatred and violence that dwell in the human heart. Let us mourn the ways in which the peoples of the world mistrust one another. Let us mourn the injustice that is so prevalent in our world and so often leads to acts of terrorism. Let us this day mourn the fallen state of humanity.

And then let us come to the table where we are reminded that the God we have come to know through Christ is a God who suffers humanity's violence with us so that we can see what divine love looks like. Let us come to the table where we are reminded that the God we know through Christ is a God of resurrection, able to take the most horrific of human acts and use them to bring about inexplicable hope.

My friends, we have come to the day many of us perhaps have expected even though we wished for it not to come. As we embark on this difficult and dangerous road, may we encourage one another and pray for one another, and may God give us and our nation's leaders the wisdom and the peace that surpasses human understanding. Amen.

In the days following 9/11, there was an eerie silence. I hadn't realized how accustomed I was to the sound of airplanes passing overhead until there weren't any, for all the airlines were grounded. Across the globe, people shared our shock and grief and expressed their solidarity with the people of the United States in the face of this atrocity.

The days after the terrorist attacks felt pregnant with possibility to me. Shocked and rocked as we were with grief, our world had been ripped open, and any number of outcomes was possible. Would the atrocity of this act awaken us to the senselessness and deplorable nature of violence and challenge us to discover more innovative ways to respond?

Would we have the humility to seek out the people who might help us find a constructive way forward? Convene a gathering of Nobel Peace Prize winners, people like Nelson Mandela and the Dalai Lama, who could help us map a path to peace? Would we ask the people of the world to join us in a period of mourning for all those who had lost their lives through war, oppression, and senseless violence? Would we put out a call to the artists of the world to give expression to our collective shock and grief and help us heal? Would we boldly lead the world toward a new path? Or would we blindly follow the script of violence that had been so devastatingly delivered to us that sunny September morning?

It soon became clear what direction we would pursue. All voices calling for the situation to be examined from a broader perspective and to examine the roots of the attackers' hatred toward the US were vehemently silenced. The media became a megaphone for an administration bent on revenge. On World Communion Sunday, the war in Afghanistan began.

My friend Christine had started asking her friends to keep her family in our prayers. Her father had not been seen since the morning of September 11th and they didn't know what had become of him. Like the thousands of people posting fliers with pictures of their loved ones on walls and light poles all over New York City, Christine and her family were trying desperately to track down her father.

Days passed and still there was no word of him. Eventually their worst suspicions were confirmed. They heard that he had left home that morning to meet a friend for breakfast at a restaurant in the World Trade Center.

Although she dreaded it, Christine knew she would have to make a pilgrimage to the place where he had died.

She had to see it with her own eyes. She asked me and a couple of other friends to come with her to Ground Zero.

We left Philadelphia early in the morning and drove to New York City, to a ferry terminal on the banks of the Hudson where the Red Cross had set up a facility for those who had lost loved ones. When we arrived, dozens of people were already milling about, anxiously awaiting the ferry that would take us downriver to the site that was still closed off to the public.

While we waited to board the ferry, Red Cross Volunteers moved through the crowd distributing breathing masks, which they urged us to wear when we disembarked. They also passed out teddy bears, which I found offensive—it seemed like a trite gesture, given the gravity of the situation. Out of courtesy, however, I accepted the stuffed bear the volunteer handed me.

Once we had boarded the ferry it slowly pulled away from the terminal and headed down the Hudson. The city's gleaming skyline glided by us in the bright autumn sun.

When we disembarked, we walked the short distance to the place where the towers had stood and filed up onto the temporary wooden viewing platform.

I was completely unprepared for what I saw. The television images had been pale snapshots compared to the magnitude of the devastation. Desperate for comfort, I clutched my teddy bear against my chest, understanding now the genius of the Red Cross's gift.

Tears streamed down my face as I took in the cavernous, smoldering wasteland, this enormous, terrible wound. A grief rose up in me larger even than the gaping chasm before me. It was a grief not just for Christine, her father, and the thousands of other lives that had been shattered and lost here. It was a grief for our entire species, for all the suffering we had caused because of our captivity to a narrative of violence that was so antithetical to the loving, unified Reality I had recently beheld.

We returned to the ferry, and as we started upriver again, a therapy dog made his way through the crowd. An earnestly friendly golden retriever, he seemed to know exactly what we humans needed. His tongue hanging out of his smiling mouth, he looked up into the faces of the shocked passengers with deep brown eyes, his tail gently wagging. People leaned over to run their fingers through the silky fur behind his ears and under his chest, comforted by his innocent presence.

When we got back to the Red Cross terminal, volunteer massage therapists were offering foot massages. I went with Christine and our companions into the section partitioned off with curtains. Taking off my shoes and socks, I lay down on one of the massage tables.

Without saying a word, the volunteer began to gently massage the pressure points on the soles of my feet. Tears streamed down my temples again as the images of what I had just seen flooded my mind. But the tears of shock and grief were now mingled with something else: tears of gratefulness for this stranger who was touching my feet with such compassion, expecting nothing of me in return.

Chapter 13: Saying Yes to Raven

A deep sense of relief came over me as Gwen and I drove past the towering red cliffs near the entrance to Ghost Ranch in northern New Mexico. For a year my soul had been desperately thirsty for this dry land.

Ghost Ranch was a place I knew well. I had taught Spanish there for several summers after my return from Ecuador. I had always found it to be a healing place; something about its arid spaciousness cleansed me of grief.

As we pulled off the highway the familiar land came into view—mesas, cliffs, sandstone pillars. It was just as I had remembered it. I felt comforted by the fact that even though change and loss had swept through my life, this land had remained the same.

Gwen and I had come on retreat to mark the first anniversary of Tricia's death. I was grateful for Gwen's companionship—for her quiet spirit, her intuitive insight, her extraordinary ability to listen.

After we settled into our rooms, we had dinner and then went to bed early. That night I had a dream.

I and many other people and animals are gathering outside.
It is nighttime and we are about to begin a sacred proces-
sion up a mountain. We will take turns carrying a small
dog, which, I sense, will undergo some kind of transforma-
tion or initiation when we reach the summit.

As the journey is about to begin, an old white wolf
comes to me offering his help. He is nearly blind in an
injured eye. I know that he has uncanny powers of vision
and great wisdom. He tells me he will travel with us and
assure our safe passage on this difficult and perilous journey.

In the morning over breakfast I shared the dream with Gwen.

"Do you know that in some Native American tradi-
tions Wolf is understood to be a teacher and pathfinder?"
she asked.

"No, I didn't."

I was grateful that such a wise guide had come to me
offering his help. Still, I had no idea what this initiation
might be, or what the perils were that called for White
Wolf's protection.

Since I had last been to the ranch a labyrinth had been
built. Nestled near the golden cliff of Kitchen Mesa, with
breathtaking vistas of the surrounding landscape, its path
was outlined with flagstones and smooth black river stones.
Large boulders rested in its center.

One morning I went there carrying a small collection
of stones, an offering of thanks for Tricia's friendship. When
I reached the center of the labyrinth I bowed to the four
directions, taken by the breathtaking beauty of the land all
around me. As I placed the stones on the ground I noticed a
card someone had left: "With God the end is never an end,
but only a new beginning."

As I turned to begin my walk back out of the labyrinth,

a gust of wind came up, blowing the card onto the path. When I walked by it I stopped to read it again: "With God the end is never an end, but only a beginning." A moment later another gust of wind blew the card into the sagebrush at the edge of the labyrinth. When I went to look for it, it was gone.

One night before going to sleep I posed a question to Tricia, asking her what she knew now that she wanted me to know. That night I had a dream that left me deeply troubled.

I am milling around in a crowd at an outdoor event, maybe a grand opening of some kind. As I walk around I notice some enormous footprints in the concrete side-walk that are unlike anything I have ever seen. They look foreboding, a sign that some otherworldly presence is approaching. No one else in the crowd seems to notice them except for one man, dressed in a trench coat. I know he is an undercover agent for the government. He realizes the footprints are heralding something ominous and he is on his cell phone trying to alert his superiors.

Now all the people have been evacuated and it is nighttime. I am with a friend in an outdoor food court enclosed by an iron fence with a locked gate. We've ordered fast food and now we have to pay for it, but we don't have the money. My friend knows the code for an ATM machine here and we are able to pay and get out.

Now I'm walking in the mountains in wintertime, approaching a fancy ski resort that has recently opened. I am dumbfounded that they have gone ahead with this project even though the footprints have already begun to appear. I am certain that the hubris behind building such a resort will lead to disaster.

I approach the main building, watching the oblivious people clumsily snowplowing across the powdery snow. I wonder if I should sell all of my stocks before this entire venture collapses, taking the economy with it and leading to mass panic.

I go into the lodge to see the woman, Enoa (pronounced: ee-no-way), who was the driving force behind building the resort. She is hurrying to a ceremony where she is about to be honored. Enoa is self-assured, fashionably dressed, confident, and ambitious. Even though I know they have made a disastrous mistake in building this resort, I congratulate her on her accomplishment.

Behind her is a wall of stained-glass windows. As we speak I am horrified to see the windows begin to take on the shape of the enormous footprints I saw before. I know that the power, whatever it is, has arrived in full force and this whole arrogant human enterprise is doomed.

Enoa gives the order to deploy the airbags that had been installed on the exterior of the building to protect it from such a catastrophe. I am incredulous that they actually think they could manufacture something that would protect us from this force. I know that their efforts are naïve and futile, and that it is now too late. A booming voice resounds throughout the building: "Fire Enoa, champion or not."

Now I am looking out over a valley with mountains in the far distance. In the foreground is a hut with a small girl standing next to it. The landscape doesn't look real. It looks like a child's drawing, and the small girl like a stick figure. I wonder if the people in this remote area will be safe from the ominous power that is taking over the world. As I look out over the valley a voice narrates a message to me.

"Traditionally, the people lived in small wisdoms. When winter came it was time to change all that."

I sense that "wisdoms" refers to the villages where

the people lived, and that now they are spending half of the year in larger communities.

"The children spent their days trying to believe that thirst was a natural part of being alive. Our dragon was known to be the kindest, most generous with the water."

Horrified, I suddenly realize what has happened. Dragons have taken over the land and have taken control of the water supply, rationing it out, and the children are living their lives in constant thirst.

I woke from the dream with my heart pounding, feeling a deep sense of foreboding about the future of the world. I desperately wanted to understand the dream's message.

What did the dragons that were taking over the world symbolize? What was the "fast food" that now had to be paid for, and what was the code for the ATM? What ill-fated plans were being driven by human ambition that would lead to catastrophe and economic collapse? What did it mean that Enoa needed to be fired, "champion or not"? And what might the coming winter be that would force people to leave their small wisdoms behind?

I didn't know. All I knew was that the dream filled me with dread. It seemed like Tricia was warning me of some impending catastrophe, and I was left struggling to know what my role was in trying to avert it.

I had brought with me on retreat a drawing Tricia had given me for my fortieth birthday of a dark-haired woman cloaked in the body of a raven, one of her wings outstretched. On the back of the drawing she had written me a message, saying that Raven presages a change in consciousness, granting a woman the courage to enter the Great Mystery, the Void of all that isn't yet in form.

On the last day of my retreat, after Gwen had returned home, I took a hike. A raven was flying overhead, catching the currents of air along the face of a cliff. Watching it, I felt within the same fierce resolve I had had after Tricia's death, when I knew I wanted to go deeper into the nature of my existence.

"Raven," I said, "I'm ready." Ready to enter the Mystery, the Void, the change in consciousness.

The following morning, as I was driving slowly down the dirt road exiting the ranch, a large raven approached, flying low along the road towards me. At the last moment, just before it reached my car, it veered away to the west.

Chapter 14: El Salvador

I craned my neck to take in the view as we began our descent into San Salvador, flying over lush volcanic peaks. The evening sun cast a rainbow halo around the plane's shadow as it glided across the towering thunderclouds.

I thought about how much this tiny country had influenced my life, even though I had never set foot in it. My first year in seminary I had helped translate into English the accounts of people who had been tortured by the military regime during the war, recounting cruelties no human being in their right mind could ever perpetrate and no human being should ever have to endure. Maybe it was because of those stories that I knew I couldn't simply stand by when, in the fall of my second year, six prominent Jesuit priests, professors at El Salvador's University of Central America, were brutally assassinated. On November 16, 1989, members of a right-wing death squad had entered their university dormitory during the night and viciously slain them, along with their housekeeper and her daughter.

The Jesuit community in the Bay Area organized a prayer vigil and act of civil disobedience to demand a halt to the US government's support of the Salvadoran regime. I and many others joined them. Gathering on the sidewalk in front of the Federal Building in San Francisco, 1,500 of us dressed in black—most wearing crosses, many wearing clergy collars—prayed and sang. Office workers in the government high rise across the street looked on, some of them looking pensive, others holding up signs against the windows telling us to go home.

After our time of prayer, those of us who were willing to risk arrest moved to the front of the building and formed a cordon around it, blocking the entrance. We knelt down on the concrete terrace and began singing chants of the Taizé community.

Jesus, remember me, when you come into your kingdom,
Jesus, remember me, when you come into your kingdom.

I was kneeling in front of the plate glass window of the lobby, where a large bronze seal of the United States hung on the opposite wall. Reflected in the window, I could see the line of kneeling protestors, and behind us the police in riot gear, the dark shields of their helmets hiding their faces.

Soon the arrests began, starting with the people directly in front of the entrance. The police came behind them, pulled them to their feet, handcuffed them, and took them into the building.

Ubi caritas et amor. Ubi caritas, Deus ibi est. Where Love is, God is.

As they continued making the arrests, the singing to my right became fainter and fainter. My knees, resting on the hard concrete, began to ache.

Stay with us, oh Lord Jesus Christ, night will soon fall.
Then stay with us, oh Lord Jesus Christ, light in our darkness.

The person next to me was pulled up and led away, and I heard one of the police officers say over his walkie-talkie, "Okay, the doors are clear."

I was aghast that they intended to declare the protest over and simply resume business as usual. Before even thinking about it, I stood up, moved over in front of the door, and knelt down again to keep the protest going. One of my classmates joined me. Immediately, an irate officer yanked me to my feet, pulled my arms hard behind my back, tightened the plastic cuffs around my wrists, and led me inside to the elevator.

When we reached the floor where the jail cells were, the elevator doors opened and a wave of music washed over me. From their cells nuns, priests, and seminarians were singing, their powerful song reverberating loudly off the concrete walls.

Digo sí, Señor, en tiempos buenos y en tiempos malos.
I say yes, my Lord, in all the good times and all the bad times.

I had never felt anything like it—this power that had nothing to do with guns or bars or handcuffs. I knew beyond all doubt it was more potent than any worldly power could ever be.

I was led to one of the cells, and as I stepped in I joined my voice with the others: "*Digo sí, Señor, en tiempos buenos y en tiempos malos.*"

The door clanged behind me, and I had never felt so free.

We landed in San Salvador just as the moon was rising. That night, after we had gone to bed, the heavens opened up with lightning, crashing thunder, and a torrential tropical rain.

By morning the storm had passed over and we awoke to sunshine, fresh air, and the song of hundreds of birds singing outside the hotel courtyard.

I had come with a delegation of people from Philadelphia congregations, including Tabernacle, that had a partnership with a small village in El Salvador settled by people who had been displaced by the Salvadoran civil war. We spent our first few days visiting some of the places that had been pivotal during the war and meeting with those who were continuing the struggle for justice.

We first met with women community organizers who told us their heart-wrenching stories of being captured and tortured by the military during the war. Afterward we spoke with a labor union member about what was happening in the country as a result of "free trade." Labor unions were being crushed and the public service sector—telecommunications, health, education—were being privatized, handed over to corporations for profit. The national government was even paving the way for transnational corporations to take over the water supply.

The foreboding dream I had had on retreat in which dragons—symbols of ruthless greed—had taken over the water supply was already coming true. What was remarkable was that the people of El Salvador, believing that they could take on these dragons and win, were organizing.

The following day we traveled to Sinquera, a small town that had been a hub of the resistance during the civil war.

After taking a hike through the rain forest to visit some of the places where the guerrillas had had their camps, we returned to the town and listened to one of the village elders tell his story. A gifted storyteller, he had us spellbound recounting a time during his youth when a new priest came to town.

"Before, just about everyone in our area was illiterate and very poor," he said. "We had no shoes. Many times we went to bed hungry. And we believed that our poverty was the result of our own personal failures, because that's what we'd been taught! But then a new priest came to our village and everything began to change. He started teaching us how to read, using the Bible as our text. And oh how our eyes were opened! We started to learn about God's burning desire for justice for the poor and oppressed. And for the first time we began to realize that sin wasn't just a personal thing. Sin could take shape in systems, in unjust systems. That's when we started to understand that our poverty wasn't the result of our personal sins. It was the result of an immoral political and economic system!"

His tale reminded me of the Quichua Indians I had known in Ecuador, whose encounter with the gospel had led them to similar feelings of empowerment and worth.

That evening those of us from Tabernacle met with José, one of the people Tab had sheltered during the days of the Sanctuary movement, and the next day we went to the Universidad Centroamericana.

It was here the Jesuit priests, their housekeeper, and her daughter had been massacred. The priests had been renowned liberation theologians and outspoken advocates for the poor. When the assassins came in the middle of the night, they shot the priests in the head to symbolize the destruction of their ideas. Then they dragged their bodies down the narrow hallway and discarded them in the courtyard garden to be discovered the next day.

I had heard the account of what happened on that terrible night, an event that finally turned the tide of popular opinion in the United States against our government's ongoing support of the Salvadoran military. But being here, seeing the simplicity of the priests' dormitory rooms, the corridor they had been dragged down, the small, grassy garden where their bloody bodies had been left made it all horrifyingly real.

While we were touring the university museum, where artifacts and photos telling about each of the priests were on display, Jon Sobrino walked through. I knew of Sobrino from my seminary studies. He was a well-known theologian whose life had been spared because he happened to be out of the country the night his colleagues were massacred. I couldn't imagine what it must have been like for him to have been the lone survivor.

We left the university and headed to the place where Archbishop Oscar Romero had been assassinated. I couldn't help but notice the number of murals depicting his image as we drove across the city.

A conservative, acquiescent bishop when he was first appointed archbishop of El Salvador in 1977, Romero's appointment was welcomed by the oligarchy of fourteen wealthy families that had controlled the country since the early 1800s. But when a close friend of Romero, Father Rutilio Grande, who had been ministering to the poor and working for their empowerment, was assassinated by military death squads, Romero became radicalized. Despite the dangers to his own life, he began to speak out publicly against the government's violence and oppression, demanding that the military cease the repression. Knowing that his own life was in jeopardy, he prophetically said that if he were to be killed he would rise again in the Salvadoran people.

One day, presiding over Mass in a small hospital chapel near his apartment, Romero was lifting the chalice during the Eucharist when an assassin shot and killed him.

When we arrived at the small, bare, two-room apartment where Romero had lived, I felt I was walking on holy ground. On display in glass cases were his scant possessions, among them his Bible and the blood-stained cassock and vestments he had been wearing when he was killed.

But it was his eyeglasses that pulled me toward them.

Standing in front of the glass case and gazing at them, I felt as though they were conveying something to me. These were the lenses through which Romero had seen the world, and what he saw had changed him. It was his willingness to *see*, and to speak about he saw, that was the courageous act for which he ultimately paid with his life.

After visiting many of the sites that had been significant during the war, our delegation drove to the remote village of Las Anonas, our sister community. Upon our arrival we were welcomed warmly and served a generous meal in an open-air shelter as stray pigs and chickens grazed in the adjacent field.

We had come mostly to deepen the long-standing relationship between our communities. At night we stayed with families in the village and during the day met with community leaders to learn about the challenges they were facing.

On our first evening we attended Mass in the unadorned, cinder block sanctuary of the village church. Parishioners sat on metal folding chairs. Now and then a mangy dog would wander through, or a toad, attracted by the light, would hop in from the dark and be chased down the aisle by squealing children. Over the mayhem the priest, Father Felipe, delivered his homily.

Basing his message on Jesus's teaching about the dangers of building one's house upon the sand, Father Felipe was employing a word play. On and on he went about the dangers of building one's house on the sand of greed and materialism, repeatedly using the Spanish word for sand, *arena*, which was also the name of El Salvador's right-wing political party, ARENA.

The following evening, sitting in a circle outside the church, we met with Father Felipe. He told us more about the living conditions of the people and the current state of the Catholic church in El Salvador. He gave us a brief history of liberation theology, which had arisen in Latin America in response to brutal inequities. He asserted God's preferential option for the poor, describing poor people as a sacrament of God.

Just as Father Felipe was saying this, Don Nicolás, the oldest man in the village, approached, humped over and shuffling slowly, walking stick in hand, wearing his frayed straw hat, a machete dangling from his belt. Father Felipe stopped mid-sentence and said, "Let us pause for a moment. Here comes a sacrament of God." We all fell silent for a holy moment as Don Nicolás passed by.

On the minds of many people while we were there was the Salvadoran government's deliberations over whether or not to sign the Central American Free Trade Agreement with the United States. CAFTA would extend NAFTA's trade guidelines into Central America, and there was widespread disagreement about whether or not this would benefit Salvadorans.

For those of us visiting from Philadelphia there was no question. This treaty would benefit the wealthy elite of the country and do little for the common people. The influx of corporate agriculture would make it harder for small farmers to survive, and CAFTA would undermine the sovereignty of El Salvador, since corporations would be able to sue the government if it instituted laws, including environmental protections, that might reduce corporate profits.

Our delegation held a press conference to speak about this issue. Several television, radio, and newspaper journalists showed up, interested to hear our perspective. As one of the few fluent Spanish speakers in the group, I was designated to be one of our spokespeople.

"Our city of Philadelphia was once a great center of

manufacturing jobs," I said into the microphone in front of me. "But now the city is full of 'bombed out' areas—miles upon miles of abandoned factories and decimated neighborhoods—and our unemployment rate is one of the highest in the country. Why? Because the factory owners moved to places where labor was cheap. CAFTA seems to promise good jobs, but very few will actually be created, and the profits will go overseas. The corporations that want to locate here will demand that your government build new highways and infrastructure so they can easily ship their goods, but it will come at the expense of basic services the people need, like education and health care. And if the workers here try to organize to demand better wages or working conditions, the corporations will simply relocate again, to where they can pay their workers less. This treaty will subsidize the rich and leave the poor to struggle in the shadows."

That evening our press conference appeared as one of the lead stories on the nightly news. Because it was illegal in El Salvador for foreigners to speak out about political issues, we had been strategic about when we held the press conference; we were leaving the next day, and knew that by the time our actions came to the attention of the officials we would be gone.

Not surprisingly, despite our efforts and the hundreds of thousands of Salvadoran citizens who demonstrated in opposition to the privatization of public services, the ARENA-led Salvadoran government went on to ratify CAFTA in 2006.

My trip to El Salvador brought to the forefront of my mind again the injustice of imperialism and the suffering it causes. With its turbulent history and present struggles, the name of that crucified little country seemed that much more poignant: El Salvador. The Savior.

Being in Latin America brought into sharp focus for me how, after 9/11, our country had been in a sort of hypnotic trance. Reality was being manufactured for us in the highest echelons of power. The patriotism that had swept across the country after the terrorist attacks was being harnessed by political leaders with imperialistic ambitions promoting messianic stories about the United States being in a war against evil.

Because of their history, the people of El Salvador could see through such propaganda. Being among them was like stepping out of a contrived fantasy and into the clear light of day.

Chapter 15: The Dawning

After my trip to El Salvador things started getting strange. For one thing, a dream I had had in seminary came to the forefront of my mind, as though the time had come for me to finally understand its message. It was a dream I had had while visiting Kip, Tricia, and Stephen over Thanksgiving during our internship year. I had never been able to decipher it, even though I knew it was the most important dream I had ever had.

A powerful woman—an otherworldly, archetypal woman—has just shapeshifted into form. I realize she is a dire threat to the world and she must be stopped. There is no one else here to do it. It's up to me.

I intend to destroy her with spiritual power. I run over and stand before her. I raise my right arm above my head to gather energy, my eyes roll back. Then I bring my arm down and point it at her, looking her in the eye.

Her eyes lock onto mine. She has tremendous power. It envelops me, paralyzes me. I am helpless. I realize now that I can never defeat her. She is far too powerful. Now all I want is to survive the encounter.

Somehow knowing what this confrontation is really about, I say to her, "I don't need personal strength because God's strength lives in me."

"Oh yeah?" she says. "Soon you will know no one."

I am terrified. She is casting a spell on me. Cursing me to be cast out into an eternal void where I will be utterly and forever alone.

I jolted awake from the nightmare with my heart pounding.

For years this dream had haunted me. Who was this woman? Why did she challenge my claim that I didn't need personal strength because God's strength lived in me? What did she mean that I would soon know no one? Had she truly been evil, as I had thought her to be? Or was that simply the sexism I had internalized that told me that powerful women are demonic?

As the dream returned to my awareness, I began to question the nature of power. Does all power belong to the divine—as I had seemed to believe in the dream—or do humans share in that power? Suddenly this seemed like a critical question I needed to answer, and it brought to mind a conversation I had had shortly before leaving for El Salvador.

I was sitting with my friend Sara in her garden on the summer solstice. She was pointing to a circle she had drawn on a sketch pad, explaining the five elements of Chinese medicine and how energy flows through systems.

"At the bottom of the cycle is winter. It corresponds to the element of water. It's the season of darkness and rest, when the aquifers replenish themselves and new possibilities begin to coalesce under the surface. Then, in spring, the energy starts to move upward into the element of wood—like the woody stems of plants—which provides the structure for the energy to continue flowing upward into the element of fire. Fire is summer, which is also associated with the heart. It is joy, love, and community." She gestured to another part of the drawing. "This upward motion is the yang part of the cycle. Then comes the yin. In late summer the energy begins to descend. This is the season when the fruits of summer are distributed, and it corresponds to the element of earth. The energy continues moving down into autumn, the season of letting go—which is also associated with grief—before it pools again in water, and the cycle begins again."

Sara and I had met the year before in a small women's spirituality group that had formed a few months after Tricia's death. Although she was best known as an accomplished watercolor artist, Sara was also well versed in Chinese medicine and the acupuncture points.

As I sat listening to her, something in me lit up. She was describing something I had always intuitively known about my work but had never had a way to articulate: *ministry was about shaping and directing energy.*

I remembered two years before, when I had been writing the letter to our church council introducing the idea of the Arts and Spirituality Center, how singularly focused I had been. Every cell in my body was vibrating with YES! I could *feel* this vision already happening. In that precise moment the Tab can on my desk had begun to leak.

Could it be that the intensity and singular focus of my own energy had caused the can to leak?

As this question was rolling around in my mind a few days later, an offhand comment Sara had made prompted me to pull one of Kip's books off our bookshelf—a book about Wicca. As I began reading it, I learned that personal power is one of the essential aspects of Wicca. Wiccans believe that energy can be harnessed and directed to bring forth a particular goal.

I realized now that my comment to the woman in the dream that I didn't need personal strength because God's strength was in me revealed two things about what I believed: God and I were separate; and God had power and I didn't.

The woman in the dream challenged that belief. She proclaimed that the time would come when I would know *no one*. I would come to understand that there was no such thing as an individual, a "one" cut off from all else. Nor was there any separation between me and God. At the time I had taken the woman's words to be a terrifying curse, but maybe they had been a blessing, promising a profound shift in my understanding.

Unbeknownst to Sara, she continued to say and do things that were helping me unlock the message of my dream. When I decided to hunt down my journal from seminary so I could re-read my account of the dream, I was blown away to see that I had had the dream on Sara's birthday, eleven years before we had met. How was this possible, that I had had the most important dream of my life on the birthday of the person who was helping unlock its meaning all these years later? The synchronicities were causing my world to crack apart. I was falling through the looking glass into a different reality where the rules of causality didn't apply. I felt as though I were a character in a magical realist novel being written by some unseen hand.

I didn't know what was happening. All I knew was that I needed to surrender to it, and that I needed to go to the woods to do it.

It was a Friday afternoon in late July, hot and humid. As I began my hike into the woods a light rain started to fall. I headed for a secluded place I knew where I sometimes went to meditate, and sat down on a large rock overlooking the Wissahickon Gorge. The branches of a nearby oak sheltered me as the rain began to fall harder.

I didn't know what to do. All I could think of was to give thanks for all the people in my life. I sensed that whatever was happening to me was happening because of my web of relationships.

I turned my face to the sky.

"Thank you for Sara. Thank you for Gwen . . ."

As soon as I started naming the names, a sudden realization flooded my being: I was not a discrete self, isolated in my own existence, as I had always perceived myself to be. I was a dynamic pattern, constantly changing, expressing the interplay of an infinite number of interacting influences, like ripples constantly dancing and colliding on the surface of water.

In a flash I comprehended not only the interconnectedness of reality but of *my own* interconnectedness with reality. "I," as a separate entity, did not exist; isolation and separateness had only been erroneous ideas in my mind.

With that realization, waves of energy began to cascade through my body, pulsating through me. I sobbed and sobbed and sobbed. I could feel that something was being set free at the deepest levels of my being. I was being birthed into a new reality.

As the waves of energy began to subside, the rain began to let up. When I opened my eyes, I saw a world I had never seen before.

Everything—the pool of tears at my feet, the rock, the trees, the sparkling, mica-laden soil—*everything* was vibrant and alive, luminous, infused with a presence. No, not merely a presence—a *Sentience.* Nothing was inanimate. Everything was expressing a Life, a Totality, a complete Oneness: Love itself.

Beholding the beauty of all that was around me, an immense hope for the Earth filled my being. I knew that a profound shift was underway, not just in me but across the entire planet. I had no doubt that if enough people were to give themselves over to this in-breaking of Love, the Earth itself could be healed.

Chapter 16: The Dream Exposed

For the next several days the hot, tingling energy continued to flow through my arms and hands. The calluses
on the soles of my feet began to peel. I continued in a state of
heightened consciousness, needing only two or three hours
of sleep each night.

I felt giddy. The world, all caught up in its fear and
drama about things that were so clearly figments of pure
imagination, seemed hilarious to me. Equally hilarious was
seeing how oblivious people were to their true nature. They
actually believed they were the roles they were playing in
this life, not timeless expressions of the totality of all Being.
I felt as though I were privy to a private joke.

And it wasn't only my mind that had awakened—it
was also my heart. I was filled with an ecstatic joy, feeling
a deep rapport with everything around me, delighting in
the sentience within all things. I was in Love. Each night
I awoke around two o'clock, rose, and went to my desk to
journal by candlelight. One night I wrote about my trolley trip into Center City the day before. Waiting on the

underground platform, I looked at the people around me. They were all in a trance, sleepwalking, lost in the maze of thoughts playing out in their minds.

> *The people are asleep! They can't see! They are caught in the illusion of individualism. They think they are alone. Separate. They're not! We're not! It's all a web. Energy. Matter. Pulsating. Vibrating. Sending ripples. Out, out, out. It's all connected! One fabric!*
>
> *The reign of God. This is the reality, the realm Jesus was <u>always</u> talking about!*

Over the coming days insights continued to pour forth, and I continued to wake and rise in the middle of the night to write. My mind was racing, synapses on overdrive. I could see now that the reality I had once believed in was nothing but an illusion—and what I would have believed to be delusional before was revealing itself as Reality. What was happening to me? Was I losing my mind?

> *When I step back and look at all this it seems like I must be going crazy. But maybe I'm becoming sane. Breaking loose from the insanity of the world.*
>
> *. . . Red alert! Red alert! Paradigm meltdown. Destruction imminent! Evacuate immediately! Get the <u>hell</u> out of this nightmare illusion, this deception. This Disneyland! It's <u>not</u> real!*

The Bush administration had just begun to make public its plans to invade Iraq, which gave this unfolding awareness a tremendous sense of urgency. At some point the word "story" began repeating itself over and over in my mind like a soundtrack beneath all my thoughts.

["Story"] I had a thought about calling Jesus by his Hebrew name—Yeshua. ["Story"] Give him back to the Jews, to his people. ["Story"] Yeshua. Savior. Yes. Savior . . . Saving us from our illusions, deceptions. ["Story"]

Did some cosmic shift truly happen when he was crucified? ["Story"] Maybe so. And the shock waves are moving out over the centuries. ["Story"] We're feeling them now.

But maybe not just him. ["Story"] With the Buddha too. Mohammed. Gandhi. ["Story"] Those who see the realm. See the Reality . . . ["Story"] They shake the foundations. The structure of the deception. ["Story"]

Now I get it why Jesus wouldn't have it ["Story"] when people wanted to worship him or make him king. ["Story"] Get off it! You're missing the point! Hello?!?! It's about all of us being this reality. ["Transform"]

The soundtrack had suddenly skipped to a new word *["Transform"]*, which played itself over and over and over again *["Transform"]*, like a mantra that had claimed my mind *["Transform"]* to chant itself into being. *["Transform"]*

Then, in a flash, the two words collided, like two chemical compounds combining with an explosive message, an urgent mandate: *TRANSFORM STORY!*

I could suddenly see what was generating and feeding the illusory world. It wasn't binary code, like in the movie *The Matrix*, but *story*. And the story humans were enacting was built upon one fundamental error: separateness. It was this erroneous *story* that was decimating the Earth, promulgating warfare and impoverishing the masses. It was a story that contained the seeds of our own destruction.

The message, which seemed to come from another dimension, was emphatic: *The time is now! Change this story!!!*

I wrote as fast as I could to try to keep up with the information that was pouring forth.

We're living in a <u>story</u>! And when we comprehend that, then we can alter it! Like a lucid dream. If we're conscious, we can help <u>shape</u> the narrative.

Above my desk was a reproduction of one of Sara's paintings, *Alterpiece*. It was a visual depiction of what was happening to me—a dynamic, living presence was penetrating the foundations of an old story.

How do we engage the narrative? Wake up from it, step outside it, so as to alter it through our awareness? How to become lucid? Engage it symbolically? Mythically? Step outside its rules for how we are supposed to engage? Take back the story? Adhere to different rules <u>altogether</u> . . . How do we become the <u>authors</u> of this story? Not just characters in it?

    It's time we become the <u>authors</u>. Take back our imaginations. Our power. Write a new narrative. Transform the <u>Story</u>!!!

I realized that our fear of death was at the heart of the domination story we were enacting, but death, too, was just part of the illusion.

We're matter—which is Energy. You can't kill energy!

I knew, too, that this awakening had to do with more than just human beings.

The Universe is trying to wake up in us!!! Be roused from its slumber. Become conscious!!!! In <u>us</u>!

Suddenly something Sara had recently said to me came to mind. She was telling me about a dream she'd just had in which I had said to her, "Reality follows intention."

The full impact of the statement hit me now. Like the quantum void, the Universe is filled with unlimited possibilities that need something to coalesce onto in order to manifest, and the something they coalesce around is intention.

My thoughts continued to accelerate, gaining momentum, as though I were in a particle accelerator gaining speed in order to shatter the last vestiges of the illusion and reveal the fundamental essence of things beneath it.

With our intentions, we were *creating reality*.

With that, another tremendous rush of energy flooded through my body and the last remnants of the illusion flew apart, exposing a single, shocking awareness:

WE ARE IN A DREAM!

Everything I had been experiencing seemed to culminate with this insight, as though all vectors converged on this one simple fact.

The frenzy instantly dissipated, replaced by an energized calm. I could see so distinctly that we were living in a dream, that Bush's plans to invade Iraq were part of this dream, and that once people became aware of that they could become lucid dreamers, able to interpret events by their symbolism and engage and alter the narrative as proactive, conscious protagonists.

We're caught in the newspapers' narrative. We have to see the <u>underlying</u> narrative. The Meta News. The <u>Mythic</u> Story. <u>That's</u> where the transformation happens.

Others, I'm sure, have known this. But it's the hundredth monkey. There's a point where enough people are awake for the shift to occur. One by one, we're waking.

131

I now understood my dream about dragons taking over the land and the water supply in an entirely different way. Like the drawing of the crone and the maiden, in which both figures are simultaneously present, its meaning had suddenly flipped to something that had been there all along; I had just been unable to see it.

Only in the mythology of the West did dragons symbolize greed, hoarding, and destruction—the unrestrained drives of the ego. In Eastern mythology, dragons brought blessing, good fortune, and transformation. They represented a force that, if respected, was benevolent. They were also believed to be lovers of water.

The dream, I now realized, was showing two very different realities. In one, unconscious ego drives take control of the world, and destruction, hoarding, greed, scarcity, and suffering are the result. This was the only meaning I had been able to see when I first had the dream.

But now I realized it was revealing an alternate reality in which the arrival of the dragons indicated the transcendence of ego. Enoa (and now I realized that her name was *a one* spelled backwards) had represented the ego drives: seeking power, wealth, status, believing she could control even the forces of nature. She was eventually "fired"—perhaps with the same potent energy that had cascaded through my body—and in her place a transcendent force had taken over, ruling the world with benevolence.

The voice in my dream had said, "The children spent their days trying to believe that thirst was a natural part of being alive." They had to *try* to believe it because their thirst was based in a falsehood, a belief that they were cut off from Source and lived in a world of scarcity. But their dragon was "kind and generous" with the water they craved.

I could see now that there were two ways of perceiving—and therefore creating—our reality: through the lens of ego, which creates an illusory dream world of fear, domination, greed, and suffering, or through the lens of indivisible Reality, which unleashes blessing, good fortune, freedom, sufficiency, and gratitude. Which world we create and inhabit is ours to choose.

Chapter 17: Wilderness Temptations

Anyone who has never been caught up in an archetypal upheaval has no idea how it messes with your head, or, more precisely, your ego. In the aftermath of the energy and consciousness opening I had experienced, I needed to be guided by spiritual teachings that understood satori, knew about kundalini, spoke openly about mysticism, knew that Buddha nature is at the heart of every person.

But instead I was trying to find my way with a religious upbringing that insisted there has only ever been— and only ever will be—one person to experience union with the All, and that person was the Brought to You from Before Time Itself, One and Only Begotten (not made) Son of God Who Sitteth on the Right Hand of God the Father Almighty from Whence He Shall Come to Judge the Quick and the Dead.

Lordy.

Now that I had seen the truth that I was not a separate self, not an I, the floodgates had opened for a new awareness, a new reality, to pour in. But my ego hadn't vanished. It had only been temporarily sidelined. Soon it not only returned but latched onto the experience I'd just had as something that made me special. Having been steeped in a religion centered on messianic expectations, my ego was telling me I was an enlightened being, a chosen one, an avatar bringing a new revelation to the world.

Yeah, right.

Fortunately, there was another part of me that knew that was nonsense. I mean, think about it. What the opening had revealed was the absolute oneness of all Reality—a oneness that made it impossible for anyone to be set apart as more special than anyone else.

I finally understood one of Jesus's parables whose meaning had always eluded me: "When the unclean spirit [read: ego] has gone out of a person, it wanders through waterless regions looking for a resting place, but not finding any, it says, 'I will return to my house [read: psyche] from which I came.' When it comes, it finds it empty, swept and put in order [read: the blissful state of emptiness; nirvana]. Then it goes and brings seven other spirits more evil [read: cut off from the Reality of Oneness] than itself, and they enter and live there; and the last state of that person is worse than the first [read: ego-inflation]." (Matthew 12: 43-45)

Several days had passed and I hadn't shared my experiences with anyone, but it was becoming more than I could carry alone. I desperately needed others to accompany me and help me manage the energy that continued to flow through my body. At times my hands and feet felt like they were on fire.

I hoped that the women in my women's spirituality group could hold this with me and support me as I underwent this transformation. I asked if we could get together right away. When we gathered that night I read what I had written in my journal. As I told them the story, every cell in me was vibrating.

But as soon as I finished, an awkward silence hung in the air, and I was filled with dread. Did they think I was crazy? Had my expectations of them been unrealistic? Had I failed to communicate what the experience had been like for me?

A few days later I told Kip and got a similar response. It seemed like the curse of the powerful woman in my dream was coming true. I felt utterly alone.

A few weeks later, Kip and I took a vacation with Stephen. On the evening of our return, I went into our office and turned on the light, startling something outside the window. I went over and discovered a bird's nest on our window ledge. Inside it were two small eggs.

The next morning, I tiptoed in to find out what kind of birds were roosting there. They were mourning doves.

Mourning doves had been my companions for many years. I had first learned their name one summer at Ghost Ranch. Their gentle cooing transported me into a sense of timelessness, and their constant presence wherever I lived had provided a thread of continuity to the many places I had called home.

Over the next weeks, I watched the male and female taking turns incubating the eggs. In early September, on the morning of my birthday, I awoke to find the eggs had hatched—two scrawny, naked birds with bobbing heads and gaping beaks. Over the next several days I watched them grow, but I soon noticed that one of them wasn't thriving. Becoming less and less able to assert itself at feeding time, it grew weaker and weaker, until one day it died.

The other, though, continued to grow. Its down gave way to feathers, and soon it was clutching the lip of the storm window frame and beating its wings, strengthening them to fly.

Meanwhile, I was preparing a ritual to honor the spiritual opening I had experienced over the summer, and I asked my women's spirituality group, along with a close friend of mine from Tucson, to join me on the evening of the fall equinox.

We gathered in the woods, under a full moon, and this time I felt their complete love and support. One by one, they anointed me and spoke their blessings for me. Some of us stayed overnight.

The following morning, when I returned home, I discovered that the bird nest was empty. The young dove had flown away.

The doves' serendipitous appearance had comforted me, conveying to me that I was being accompanied even though I felt alone in the human realm. The one dove's death seemed to symbolize the death of a former self, while the other suggested an emerging Self that would grow and one day fly.

Never having experienced energy until that day in the woods when it flooded my body, I wanted to understand more about it, so I signed up for a workshop about the energetics of healing.

The workshop was led by twin sisters, both energy workers. Afterward I asked one of them if she offered spiritual direction. She said yes, and we set a time to meet.

On the day of our first meeting I arrived early at the retreat center. Walking the grounds, I felt nervous. I didn't know how to share my experience, or how open she would be to it. Would she think I was crazy? But when I approached the retreat house to meet her, I felt relieved seeing her waiting on the porch wearing an outfit almost identical to my own.

She understood all of what I shared with her, and over the coming months her steady presence, wise guidance, and matter-of-factness about what I was going through normalized the experience for me and helped me see it within the context of our evolutionary journey.

All the while I was carrying on with my pastoral responsibilities as though nothing unusual was happening. I presided at meetings, planned and led worship services, preached, and dealt with the numerous administrative tasks involved with a church.

But inwardly, things were different. I often felt intense energy in my arms and hands when I was meditating or praying. At times during our worship services I felt a potent, numinous Presence among us. Communion in particular often transported me into the timeless Reality where there is no separation between the seen and unseen. When I lifted the communion bread to break it, I *saw* it—the tiny fissures in the crust, every line of light and shadow—as if the bread were alive and we were fully present to each other. I was awake to the fiery moment, held in the Realm of Love. It was magical.

But there were other times when I slipped back into sleep, succumbing to the gravitational pull of an old way of seeing that told me none of it was real. My inability to stay awake to the Reality I had witnessed caused me despair. I often felt like a failure.

By winter, my spiritual director encouraged me to begin receiving energy work, so I contacted Sara's friend, Zoana, who was a Reiki Master. Our Reiki sessions were profoundly healing, helping me integrate what had happened to me in recent months. Zoana, who was highly intuitive, would also receive information during our sessions that was always comforting and encouraging, reminding me over and over again that I was being accompanied.

Throughout this time, the fierce inner wrestling match continued inside me between the ego, with its hunger to be special, and the awareness of absolute Oneness that had been revealed to me. Not only had my ego latched onto its self-proclaimed specialness, it was taking on the burden that was the shadow side of that specialness: believing it had been assigned a divine mission to transform the story of planet Earth. That's a pretty tall order for an ego. A recipe for despair.

Through those difficult months there was a story in the gospels that became a lifeline for me: the story of Jesus's baptism and temptation in the wilderness. It is one of the few events of Jesus's life that appears in all four gospels, and Mark, the oldest of the four, tells it like this:

> *In those days Jesus came from Nazareth of Galilee and was baptized by John in the Jordan. And just as he was coming up out of the water, he saw the heavens torn apart and the Spirit descending like a dove into him. And a voice came from heaven, "You are my beloved son, with you I am well pleased."*
>
> *And the Spirit immediately drove him out into the wilderness. He was in the wilderness forty days, tempted by Satan. And he was with the wild beasts, and the angels waited on him. (Mark 1:9-13)*

Because the tradition I had been raised in taught that Jesus was the Christ from birth, or from the beginning of time, depending on which account you read, I had never been led to believe that this story was very important. It was sort of like his debutante's ball—the moment when he made his appearance on the public scene and the curtain was pulled back onto Act One of his ministry. His subsequent time in the wilderness was sort of like Outward Bound. He had to go off to perform a few spiritual pushups, find the inner fortitude to resist Satan's temptations to use his super-powers to his own advantage, and prove that he was up to the task he had come to do.

Now that interpretation seemed like a bunch of malarkey. Clearly something very profound had happened to Jesus at his baptism, something so unsettling that he needed to withdraw entirely by himself into the desert for "forty days"—Bible-speak for a long time.

As I read the story now, I suspected that Jesus had come to the Jordan with a singular intention: to give himself fully to God and to surrender anything that stood in the way. And since the only thing that ever stands between us and our awareness of our divine nature is the ego—our own belief in ourselves as separate entities with separate identities—Jesus relinquished himself as a self. When he came up out of the water, he had a profound awakening.

He saw heaven torn apart. The barrier of separateness between the earthly and the divine had collapsed. He could see that all was united—the eternal and the temporal, the unseen and the seen, Divinity and himself. He experienced himself as completely worthy and beloved by an Absolute Love. It was a revelation that shook him to his core.

He withdrew alone into the wilderness, and it was there that he came face to face with Satan's temptations.

Satan, the mythological personification of egotism, exemplified pride. The fallen angel, he had set himself apart from God to pursue his own cravings for adoration and power.

This was the "satanic" temptation Jesus had to confront. The nature of Reality had been revealed to him. He had seen that he was intimately related with the Source of all Being. Didn't that make him special? Wasn't it proof that he was an exception to the rest of humankind? Didn't he deserve to be worshiped? Wasn't he entitled to use power for personal gain?

No, he insisted. No, no, no. Over and over again he returned his attention to the insight he had received: God-Reality was all there was. All beings were equally part of it. The world of hierarchy and division, Satan's world, was nothing but an illusion. He understood that if he succumbed to that illusion, what he had witnessed would be lost. His awareness of Reality, of Absolute Love, would slip away again into the shadows. Asleep in the illusion, he would forget what he truly was.

Ministered to by angelic presences and accompanied by wild animals, Jesus learned during his time in the wilderness how to withstand the ego's enticements and see its deceptions clearly. Finally, he was ready to go forth to help awaken others.

As I contemplated the story, I became increasingly troubled that Jesus's specialness had become the defining belief of the religion that emerged in his name. He was *the* anointed one, set apart from all of humanity since the beginning of time. Not only that, that religion would eventually claim the same for itself: Christianity was the only true religion, the only way to God.

Despite Jesus's spiritual fortitude in the wilderness, in the end egotism had won the day. "Satan" had prevailed.

Chapter 18: Dark Night of the Ego

A year had passed since I had said yes to Raven. Since then I had seen the fallacy of separation, how that fallacy had shaped Christian belief, and how it was continuing to guide the destructive story playing out on the planet, and I had heard an emphatic message that we needed to transform that story. I urgently wanted to help, but I didn't know how.

I returned to Ghost Ranch to mark the second anniversary of Tricia's death, hoping to gain clarity about my work and to continue to attend to the process of my own spiritual unfolding.

My first day at the ranch I noticed an odd thing for the middle of winter: the ranch was crawling with tiny caterpillars. I counted them on my way to the labyrinth, giving up when I reached a hundred.

I had read that when the caterpillar goes into the chrysalis stage, its structure completely dissolves before the new being emerges. Were these caterpillars here to remind me that there was a metamorphosis underway that would follow its natural course? A process not of my own doing, yet one I could completely trust?

I came to see that I needed to let go of all of my hopes and expectations for my retreat and simply open myself to whatever wanted to come forth. As always, I ritualized my intention. I wrote down my expectations and burned them. The next day I took the ash in my prayer bowl to the labyrinth as an offering. As I was walking the winding path I received an instruction that I needed to let go of one more thing: my work.

I was shocked. Was I being told I had to leave Tab? Or was it referring to the strong sense I had, in the aftermath of my opening, that there was work I was to do to help transform our planetary story? The latter seemed like my reason for being, and the idea of letting it go was indescribably painful. Without a purpose, why live?

I didn't understand why this was being asked of me. I only knew it was necessary for some reason beyond my comprehension. So once again, I prepared a ritual. I drew a picture of the Earth encircled by rings of rainbow colors, a visual depiction of the planetary healing that was so urgently needed and that I felt so deeply called to be part of. To symbolize my work as a pastor I chose the clergy identification card I always carried in my billfold. I returned to the labyrinth that afternoon to burn them.

As I walked the labyrinth, I considered what I was letting go of. These symbols represented my calling, my vocation, my spiritual community, my place of belonging, my purpose. My heart ached. Why did the spiritual path always seem to demand that we let go of the things we most cherish?

When I reached the center of the labyrinth, I placed the Earth drawing under a rock and prepared to burn the clergy card, but the wind was too strong. I tried three times, and each time the match went out. Finally, I said, "If you want me to do this, the wind will have to die down." Instantly, it did. I lit the match and set the clergy card on fire, and then the drawing of the Earth as well.

I wept watching the image of the healed Earth become enveloped in flame, disintegrating into ash. It seemed like hope itself was being annihilated, and my own life was devoid of any purpose.

When nothing was left of the drawing, the wind picked up again, swirling the ashes up into the air and carrying them away.

That evening I tried to pray but couldn't. There was a cavernous emptiness inside me where once I had felt a passionate purpose. I felt despondent, and I went to bed early.

At three thirty I woke, still feeling a terrible void within, feeling there was no reason now for me to be here, or anywhere. I felt drawn to go for a walk, so I dressed and set out.

The desert was silent. It was a cold, clear, moonless night. Overhead the Milky Way spanned the sky, softly illuminating the distant mesas. I didn't turn on my flashlight. I walked in darkness, navigating by the light of the stars.

Eventually I ended up at the labyrinth again, though there was no reason for me to be there. I had no question to pose and nothing left to offer. It lay in stillness before me, its twisting path barely visible in the starlight.

I began to walk it. When I reached the center I bowed, as I always did, to the mesa rising up before me, a shadowy silhouette in the darkness. Just then a brilliant light peeked from the upper ridge of the mesa, piercing my eyes. Venus had risen. The morning star. Harbinger of a new day.

The light was so brilliant it blinded my night vision,

and as I walked back out I had to shade my eyes to make out the labyrinth's outline. Along the way I stopped once to look up at the blazing planet again. Just then a shooting star streaked across the sky.

The rest of my retreat was filled with a sense of buoyancy and joy, as though a weight had been lifted from me. I understood now that the message I had received wasn't meant as a literal instruction that it was time for me to resign my position at Tab. Rather, I was being asked to release all of my attachments. Any "work" that would come forth in the future wasn't to be "mine."

In the final days of my retreat, two words began to spontaneously appear in my mind, much as the words "story" and "transform" had appeared during the summer. But this time the words were "follow" and "unstoppable."

Chapter 19: Land of
the Ancestors

On my British Airways flight in late September 2003, I took care to cover up the chapter heading of the book I was reading, so the person sitting next to me couldn't see it: "Witchcraft as Goddess Religion."

I had embarked on a pilgrimage to the British Isles, where I would join a group of women to visit some of the sacred sites in England: Salisbury, Stonehenge, Avebury, Glastonbury. When I had first received the e-mail announcing the trip, I had immediately known I needed to go.

Many of the sites we would be visiting were places Tricia had explored years earlier while doing research for a novel about a modern-day woman who started to receive telepathic communications from a woman living in pre-Christian England. Taking this trip seemed like an opportunity to engage with the story she had been creating before her death.

I also wanted to go for more personal reasons. I had been struggling to sort out my relationship with Christianity. In seminary I had had to come to terms with the tradition's misogyny. Now I was faced with an even more daunting challenge: reconciling its concepts of God as a separate Other and of Jesus as someone set apart from the rest of us with what my own spiritual life had revealed to me.

I had seen the sentience and sacredness at the heart of all things. I felt a deep kinship with nature, and even things deemed "inanimate." I could sense the energetic dimension in which we all co-create reality. The biblical stories and worship liturgies that spoke of God as a Holy Other and Jesus as "His" one and only Son had begun to feel completely alien to me.

More and more I could see how Christian belief was built upon the bedrock of separation. Humans were separate from Earth, Spirit was separate from matter, Jesus was separate from the rest of us ordinary humans. These beliefs were all expressions of the ego's way of seeing the world, and they no longer held true for me.

But I couldn't just walk away, not only because I still worked in the Church but—more important—because I felt deep gratitude for Christianity and all it had given me. Despite its many flaws, it had set me on my spiritual path, and because of that I felt a sense of loyalty to it. The Church had affirmed my gifts of leadership even when I myself hadn't. The stories of the Bible were the maps that guided my life. Christianity was in my bones.

My burning question was whether I could bridge these two worlds. Could I find a way to free the religion's teachings from the influence of ego? Or was the ego perspective so endemic to the religion that there was no way to extricate it?

I hoped a pilgrimage to the land of my ancestors, to the great stone circles they had built when Earth and the Feminine had still been celebrated, would give me the missing pieces I needed to hold it all together.

When I got word of the trip I had just finished reading

a novel called *The Mists of Avalon*, a tale of the time when Christianity took over England and supplanted the Goddess religion. Glastonbury, one of the places we would be visiting, was the alleged site of Avalon. This synchronicity was one more prompt encouraging me to go.

I also considered whether I should visit Scotland while I was in the British Isles, in particular the island of Iona, where a progressive ecumenical community practiced Earth-centered Celtic Christianity. Maybe the Christianity of Iona could offer the keystone for the bridge between these worlds that I needed to build.

As the date for the trip approached and I was running out of time to decide whether to go to Scotland, I left Tab one evening to get some dinner before a meeting. Half a block away I saw something I had never seen before on the streets of Philadelphia: a man dressed in a kilt and full Scottish regalia. When he began to play his bagpipes I laughed out loud. *All right!* I thought. *I'll go to Scotland!*

En route I was trying to finish the assigned reading for the women's pilgrimage: *The Spiral Dance*, by Starhawk. It told the history of the Burning Times, when hundreds of thousands, if not millions, of people, overwhelmingly women, were subjected to horrific torture and agonizing deaths after being accused of practicing witchcraft.

As I read, it suddenly occurred to me to ask myself why I was so painstakingly hiding the chapter heading. What was I afraid of? That the flight attendant would radio ahead to the constable in London, who would be waiting at Heathrow when we landed to take me into custody and lead me to the gallows for reading a book written by a witch?

I was aghast to realize that somehow the terror of the witch hunts from centuries ago lived on in me. The unspeakable horror of that time had been quietly passed down through the generations and had lodged somewhere in the dark recesses of my psyche, where it could haunt me even while flying at 30,000 feet and enjoying my British Airways beverage.

So much of Starhawk's writing was making sense to me. The Wiccan understanding of imminence, of the aliveness of Earth. Of how energy coalesces into matter. Of our ability to engage reality in its energetic dimension and help shape it through our consciousness. These all resonated with my own perspectives.

Once we arrived in London, sans constable, I flew on to Scotland. Wandering the narrow cobblestone streets of Edinburgh, I was keenly aware of my ancestral lineage. My paternal grandmother's family was from Scotland, which was why my family was Presbyterian—the Presbyterian Church being the Church of Scotland.

In the heart of Edinburgh, along the Royal Mile, I came upon a plaque indicating the spot where they had publicly executed those accused of witchcraft. Facing unsubstantiated charges of consorting with the Devil, the accused were tortured until they confessed, and then they were executed—usually strangled and burned at the stake. The location was just a stone's throw from Saint Giles, the austere "Mother Kirk" of Presbyterianism.

I wondered what role my ancestors may have played in the persecution. Accusers? Accused? Spectators? And why was this ecclesiastical terrorism against women usually treated as little more than a footnote in history?

Visiting a nearby museum, I discovered that King James I of England, who had the Bible translated into English, had personally overseen the trial, torture, and killing of alleged witches when he was king of Scotland.

The violence the Church had perpetrated throughout the ages was horrifying. How had this happened? How had Christianity gone so awry, becoming an instrument of terror, justifying—if not instigating—genocides, the Crusades, the Inquisition, pogroms, slavery, the Trail of Tears? Could it ever redeem itself?

And how could Jesus be liberated from this gruesome legacy? Given his proclivity to side with the outcasts and the scapegoats, I had little doubt that he would have stood in solidarity with the accused, not clamored for their bodies to be tortured and their flesh burned. After all, he himself had been falsely accused, tortured, and publicly executed by political and religious authorities. Like the women who were destined for the gallows or the stake, he too was known to be a healer who accessed an invisible realm; he too was accused of consorting with the Devil.

After my unsettling day in Edinburgh I caught the train across the country to make my way to Iona, where I hoped to find a gentler Christianity.

It was already evening when the ferry approached the jetty on Iona. The green, craggy hill of the island was illuminated by the soft light of the descending sun. On the shore stood a scattering of simple houses, and beyond them Iona's stone abbey.

Several people from the Iona community were waiting on shore. They greeted us warmly, helped us with our luggage, and transported us to our accommodations.

After settling into my room, which I shared with a few other women also on pilgrimage, I made my way to the dining hall, where over dinner I talked to a man whose Scottish brogue was so startlingly thick it was hard to believe he and I were speaking the same language. Several times, I had to ask him to repeat what he had said. We laughed about how hard it was for us to communicate, but one thing that came through loud and clear was that he was deeply passionate about social justice, a passion that was obviously shared by the larger community.

That evening I went to the worship service in the medieval abbey, originally built in the twelfth century and restored in the 1930s.

Outside the abbey stood a tall, elaborately carved stone Celtic cross. While I expectantly waited for worship to begin I read about it. The cross was dedicated to Martin of Tours, who lived in the fourth century, and it had stood on Iona for twelve centuries. As a child, Martin had become interested in Christianity. As the son of an officer in the Roman army, he was obligated to serve in the cavalry when he came of age. One day, while riding through the city gates of Amiens, he saw a poorly clad beggar. Martin impulsively removed his military cloak, cut it in two, and gave half to the beggar.

That night he had a dream in which Jesus told him it was he whom Martin had clothed with his act of compassion. After this vision, Martin was formally baptized and refused to continue his service in the Roman legion. He was jailed, but was eventually released from prison and from military service.

With the disturbing legacy of Christianity's violent side still lingering in my mind, St. Martin depicted a refreshingly different story of compassion and nonviolence.

Gradually people gathered in the sanctuary, and I felt anticipation as the worship service began. I had been looking forward to this for so long, hopeful that this community I had heard about for so many years might show me a way to reconcile my worlds.

The words of the liturgy we read together were poetic, gentle, and loving, and we sang African American spirituals and lively songs from Zimbabwe. But the theology and style of worship was far more traditional than I had expected. I was shocked that the language for God was all male, and I was disheartened that there was still an assumed separation between human, divine, and nature. While nature was honored and appreciated, it still stood apart from the divine, like a painting that stands apart from the painter. Beautiful, but an object nonetheless.

I felt deeply discouraged. Had I traveled all the way across the Atlantic and the width of Scotland only to find a Christianity that was not nearly as inclusive as the Christianity we celebrated at Tab? Not even Celtic Christianity, it seemed, could offer me the spiritual home I was longing for.

After the worship service was over I sat alone in a candlelit corner of the abbey to sit with my disillusionment and to pray. During my prayer I received a message: "Do not confuse the form with the essence." The message continued, telling me I was not to confuse Jesus with the institution, or with those who claimed to speak for him and act on his behalf.

I sensed I was being told that even though the Church's forms may be antiquated expressions of an earlier age, I shouldn't let that blind me to the essence within the teachings, because that essence was important and needed to be retained. The Earth was suffering a crucifixion at the hands of ego, and although Christianity had emerged during a patriarchal and violent era and had taken on many of those characteristics, it nonetheless carried the seeds to subvert patriarchy and overcome violence. This was something I was being told not to forget.

I spent much of my time on Iona just being with the land, which, like the wind and sea, felt alive and untamed. The light, as it so often does where land meets ocean, felt numinous and filled with information.

One afternoon, while I was lying on the hillside letting the energy of the land permeate my body, I watched the sunlight dance on the rippling water as birds soared overhead and clouds glided silently and swiftly across the expanse of sky. I could understand why Rev. George MacLeod, the visionary Church of Scotland minister who had founded the present community of Iona, had spoken of this as a "thin place" where the veil between the seen and unseen worlds was permeable.

MacLeod once said, "There is no longer any such thing as dead matter. All is light-energy." His assertion that everything was alive resonated with me, but the question I continued to hold was whether Christianity could ever fully accommodate that insight. Separation between Creator and creation and a Christ who stood apart from the rest of humanity were ideas so embedded in the scriptures, doctrines, and liturgies that I didn't know how the tradition could ever move beyond them. Perhaps, like the stone walls of the island's abbey, Christianity was too rigid and enclosed to be able to expand beyond the archaic worldview that had spawned it. As Jesus himself had said, you can't put new wine into old wine skins.

Iona did not offer me the holistic Christianity I was hoping for. But it did give me other gifts, the last of which I received during the communion service the night before I left. Gathered in the candlelit abbey, the community sang together and passed the bread and wine. When I took communion I entered the dimension of timelessness and felt the spiritual Presence I often felt during communion. This time I felt it blessing me on this journey I had begun.

The next day I left Iona for London to meet up with the other women on the trip, including Anne, whom I had met through a mutual friend. Like me, Anne was an ordained clergywoman, but she was no longer serving a congregation. As we got to know each other and began to share what had been happening in our spiritual lives, we discovered we had much in common.

Our group met up at Heathrow and set out for our first stop: Salisbury. That afternoon, after we had gotten settled into our hotel room, Anne and I took a walk to Salisbury Cathedral. An architectural marvel, it looked more like a painting than a structure made of stone as we approached it across the grassy expanse of the Close. It was built in the thirteenth century and its spire, over 400 feet high, soared breathtakingly into the sky.

Formerly, when I had visited great cathedrals in Europe, I had felt a hushed reverence upon entering. The magnificent naves of vaulted stone, the jeweled light coming through stained-glass windows, the acoustics that amplified every footfall dwarfed me and left me in awe. Perhaps cathedrals were designed to evoke awe and draw worshippers into a mysterious inner realm, but this time I felt the structure severing me from Earth, cutting me off from the trees, the sky, the sunlight, and the breeze with its thick, unwavering walls. And the spire, for all its magnificence, depicted humankind's attempt to reach a deity far removed from the Earth beneath our feet.

As Anne and I walked around the sanctuary, I could see her mounting distress as well.

We left the sanctuary hurriedly and stepped into the adjacent Chapter House, a round, light, airy building where a copy of the Magna Carta was housed.

After exploring the Chapter House, we made our way to a nearby park to breathe fresh air and commune with nature.

As we walked back to the hotel it started to rain lightly, though sunlight continued to stream from the western sky. We looked to the east, and there, spanning the horizon, was a double rainbow.

The rainbow was framing a church across the street where a flock of white birds was circling. We saw that the church was named after St. Francis, patron saint of animals and the environment. The clouds then opened full force, drenching us, even as the bright westerly sun continued to shine. We burst out laughing, lifting our arms to the sky, delighted by the purifying downpour.

From Salisbury, our group visited Stonehenge and then traveled on to Glastonbury, where we stayed at an inn at the site of England's oldest well. From there we took a day trip to Avebury, where Britain's largest Neolithic stone circle stands.

Throughout the trip I felt a deepening connection to the broad sweep of history and my own place in it. I marveled at Stonehenge and Avebury and the energy I felt emanating from the land in those places. I wondered about the pre-Christian, Earth-centered cultures that had built them, and I wondered whether our break with nature had been a necessary step in our human evolution, just as adolescents have to separate from their mothers in order to come into their adulthood.

Although my trip didn't resolve my struggles with Christianity as I had hoped it would, it did bring me a sense of completion. Being with the land and the history of my ancestors, I felt as though I had traveled back to retrieve something that had been lost, something I needed for my own wholeness.

To conclude our trip, our group made a ritual hike to the top of Glastonbury's Tor. The legendary site of Avalon, the Tor is a conical hill, visible from miles around, that was once an island surrounded by wetlands. At the top stands a tower, the rebuilt ruins of one of the earliest churches in England, St. Michael's.

The wind at the top of the Tor was so fierce that I could barely stand, and I didn't linger long. But when I started walking back down again I noticed that something inside me had changed. I hadn't experienced any dramatic breakthroughs on this trip, but instead a subtle integration that had left me with a strong desire to help heal the rift between religions.

After saying good-bye to our traveling companions, Anne and I continued on to Ireland. I had asked her to accompany me there, to visit some stone circles and sacred groves and to do a healing ritual in the place where I had been raped. We spent our first night near the stone circle in Grange. From there we headed north, toward the Cliffs of Moher and Doolin.

The cliffs were as beautiful as I remembered them, emerald earth dropping away, plummeting into the undulating waves of the sea far below. As we drove on toward Doolin I became aware of my hands on the steering wheel guiding us there. Twenty years earlier I had fled this place in shock, disbelief, and shame. Now I was returning of my own free will, on my own terms, and I felt strong.

For the ritual, we drove out to a point near the water, down a road that passed by the ruins of an old church and graveyard, following the rutted road until it ended. We left the car and walked to a grassy pasture edged by a delicate, filigree-like stone wall. Though it was mostly overcast, we could see the Cliffs of Moher in the distance.

We had invited the women we had traveled with in England, as well as some friends back home, to join us at the appointed time for the ritual. As the time drew near we could feel their energy converging. Twelve women on three continents.

A couple of nights before, I had had a dream about the ritual in which I was explaining to a circle of people what ritual consciousness is. I described it as being hyper-awake and hyper-aware. Looking up and reaching out my hand,

I told them I felt as though I could touch the sky and make ripples, and as I looked at my outstretched hand I saw the sky begin to sparkle.

Anne and I proceeded in that consciousness, laying out our ritual objects on the grass, some that we had gathered and some that had been given us by our traveling companions. Then we meditated, allowing ourselves to enter a dimension in which transformation, forgiveness, and healing were already present. We held the Earth, and the turbulent human story that had caused so much suffering, in that energy of healing and forgiveness—and I held Seamus, the man who had raped me, in it as well.

We blessed the reemergence of the feminine and the reuniting of humans and Earth. To end the ritual I poured some water I had brought from the ancient well in Glastonbury onto the grass to bless the land. Just then the sun broke through the clouds and showered the nearby sea with streams of light.

Chapter 20: Questioning the Foundation

Not having found on Iona the holistic Christianity I had hoped for, I was left still wondering how I could bridge the two worlds I found myself in: the tradition in which I had been raised and now worked as a pastor, and the perspectives that had come to me in my own spiritual life.

Knowing that the biblical accounts had been skewed by egoic consciousness and that much of Christian belief had been shaped by the illusion of separateness, I wondered more and more whether I could stay in the Church. And yet the more I looked deeply into some of the accounts of Jesus's life and teachings from my new vantage point, the more I suspected the seeds of transformation might still be there, even though they'd been covered over by centuries of distorted interpretations. What was needed was a hermeneutic of consciousness, sifting through the tradition for the kernels of awakening among the chaff of ego.

Each week, as I immersed myself in the familiar gospel accounts in preparation for our worship services at Tab, I found myself noticing new things and asking many questions.

What if, by calling himself the Son of Man, Jesus was rejecting all notion of specialness and affirming that he was the offspring of all humanity, a universal human being?

What if everything Jesus did after transcending his ego identification was a revelation of *our* true nature—and the power we participate in—once freed from the ego and its illusions?

What if, when he said the Son of Man has the power to forgive sins, he was saying that humans have the capacity to set the future free?

What if Jesus silenced those who were proclaiming him the Messiah, the Son of God, because he knew this was the one idea that could derail his message? Setting him apart as special, we would alienate ourselves even further from our own true nature. Wasn't it usually the demons in the gospel stories, after all, who tried to spread that rumor?

What if Jesus's claim that the "Son of Man" would sit at the right hand of power wasn't a statement about himself as an individual but about an awakened humanity becoming a conscious, co-creative force participating in the unfolding of Life?

What if, when Jesus emerged from his baptism and perceived a unified Reality, he saw that the Roman Empire, with its centurions and crosses, was simply a falsehood, an illusion, a dream?

What if Jesus was taking on empire, not by fighting against it but by dissolving the underpinnings of its very reality?

Chapter 21: Entering the Emperor's Dream

"How do you plead?" The judge looked down at me from his bench.

"Guilty, Your Honor."

It had taken the government a year to summon those of us who had been arrested for civil disobedience when the US had invaded Iraq to appear in court.

Like millions of others, I had believed that launching a war on Iraq was not only immoral but would fuel the flames of hatred and lead to increased radicalism and terrorism throughout the world. I had written letters to the editor and to my congressional representatives and members of the UN. I had participated in peaceful demonstrations, including the historic Global Peace March, in which millions of people all across the globe flooded streets and public squares in an unprecedented demonstration for peace.

All along, though, these actions seemed insufficient to me. The dream had adapted to protests, and people demonstrating for peace were written off as "special interests."

Something different was called for now. Somehow we needed to opt out entirely of the ego's story. Instead of fighting it, we needed to make a leap of consciousness to see that empire—in fact the whole enterprise of domination—was based on nothing but illusion.

All of our efforts to avert the war had failed. The bombing of Baghdad—christened the Shock and Awe Campaign—began. On March 20, 2003, I joined hundreds of others at a historic Quaker meeting house in the heart of Philadelphia to prepare to engage in nonviolent civil disobedience at the Federal Building a few blocks away.

It was a cold, rainy morning, and the meeting house was buzzing with activity when I arrived, final preparations being made. Soon we headed en masse to the Federal Building, just two blocks from Independence Hall, where we took our places around the perimeter of the building and sat down.

A member of Tab was sitting next to me. He and I huddled together as I read passages aloud from the small Bible I had brought with me. I strained to speak loudly enough to be heard over the din of the police helicopters pounding the air above us and the angry chants of the bullhorn-wielding leader of the protesters marching in the street:

Blessed are the poor in spirit, for theirs is the kingdom of heaven. Blessed are those who mourn, for they will be comforted. Blessed are the meek, for they will inherit the earth. Blessed are those who hunger and thirst for righteousness, for they will be filled. Blessed are the merciful, for they will be shown mercy. Blessed are the pure in heart, for they will see God. Blessed are the peacemakers, for they will be called children of God. Blessed are those who are persecuted because of righteousness, for theirs is the kingdom of heaven.

The arrests began. The Federal agents started making their way around the building. When they reached us one of the marshals told us we had thirty seconds to leave or we would be arrested. When we didn't move, a young woman in uniform instructed me to stand. I stood up, reached out my hand to her and said, "Peace be with you." She took my hand and said, "And also with you." Then she handcuffed my wrists behind my back and led me inside.

When we entered the concrete tunnel into the basement of the building, we were searched and everything in our possession was confiscated. The officer who searched me noticed a lump in my pocket.

"What is that?" she demanded.

"It's my Bible."

She pulled it out to take a look, put it back in my pocket, and waved me on.

One hundred and seven people were arrested that morning in Philadelphia and held for most of the day.

When I was finally called before the judge, an officer came to the cell, handcuffed me again, and led me to the courtroom. As I entered, I felt grateful to see several Tab members in the audience. I walked to the defendant's table, sat down, and addressed the black-robed judge as I had the arresting officer.

"Peace be with you."

"And also with you," she replied.

Then she explained that we were being released on our own recognizance and would receive further instructions at a later date.

I received a letter in the spring of 2004 informing me that I could either pay a $250 fine or appear in court for a hearing. Those of us who chose not to pay the fine went to court in groups of twelve. I was in the second group, summoned to appear the Wednesday after Easter.

The courtroom was packed with supporters, among them some friends and church members, as well as my mother, who was visiting us for Easter. The defendants made their statements before the judge, many eloquent and moving, speaking about the immorality of the war and the tragic and unnecessary suffering it had inflicted. The judge, who was allowing us to speak for as long as we wanted, spent most of the time looking at his fingernails.

We knew, based on the experience of the first group that was summoned, what our punishment would be if we refused to pay the fine: seven days in maximum-security prison.

I had thought long and hard about whether to pay the fine or do the time, wondering whether going to jail would make any difference. I meditated, prayed, and consulted with Kip and others close to me, as well as several people at church, all of whom said they would support me regardless of my decision. I knew if I did go to prison, I wanted to do it with an energy of peace, not protest. In an e-mail to one of my parishioners who was helping me in my discernment process, I explained to her my reasoning:

> *[The peace movement] isn't yet truly a peace movement. It's still an anti-war movement . . . Many 'peace' activists are still living out an old role that served its purpose in its time, but it is no longer radical enough, no longer transformative enough.*
>
> *From the beginning, I felt as though the Iraq Pledge of Resistance [which I signed well before the war began] was in some ways simply playing its role of resistance in the old script. I decided to play along because I felt it was helpful for there to be visible evidence that not everyone in this country was going along with the priorities of the US*

administration. I never felt, however, that that is where the potent power of transformation lies. For me there is a much huger potential in stepping out of the script altogether and inventing together a new world, new systems. Not trying to pull out the weeds or even resist them, but to plant more vigorous and life-giving plants that will supplant the old . . . Resistance isn't where I'm at anymore. Transformation is what I long for. That is my passion.

So, what to do?? Spend a week in jail? That could be transformative for me, maybe open up opportunities to learn more about myself and the strength or deficiencies of my spiritual practices. Maybe give me a firsthand view of the prison system—the underbelly of the Beast of our society. Maybe give me practice in letting go of control, which seems to be something important at this stage in my development .

. .

[World peace] is what I yearn for most deeply. I want humans to wake up, to step out of our script in time before we mutually annihilate one another. If I go to jail, I believe the best thing I could possibly do is to spend the time in deep prayer because humanity is mad and in desperate need of healing.

I had come to see that empire was an expression of the ego, playing itself out on a global scale, and I had given shorthand terms to the two consciousnesses that were ours to choose from. "Emperor" was a term that captured for me the epitome of the ego-based mind that lived within a pseudo-reality of domination, scarcity, violence, separateness, and hierarchy. The term didn't refer to a specific individual or nation-state but rather to a thought pattern, a field of consciousness that manifested itself in tangible ways in the oppressive systems of the world.

The term "No One" captured for me the consciousness Jesus had embodied, one that transcended the ego's illusions, divisions, and drives. Like "Emperor," the term didn't refer to any specific individual or individuals but to a state of being, a consciousness that dwelled within unified Reality.

I finally decided to serve the sentence, but to do so as much as I was able with the No One consciousness of mindfulness and peace. Perhaps, like Jesus's parable of the kingdom of heaven being like a woman who hid yeast in several measures of flour, if enough people infiltrated the Emperor's strongholds with a different consciousness the world could begin to be transformed.

"Your Honor," I said, "I plead guilty. I blocked the doors of the Federal Courthouse because the gates of justice had already been obstructed in our unprovoked attack on Iraq. Since 9/11 we have allowed ourselves to be taken hostage by a narrative of violence, including the so-called 'War on Terror,' which is based on the foolish belief that violence can be annihilated by violence. When I read the news about the chaos and bloodshed in Iraq I feel deep sorrow at the needless loss of life and the terrible injustice of sending our soldiers to sacrifice themselves to return to us maimed in body and spirit. It's simply wrong."

I hadn't prepared ahead of time what I was going to say. I was just letting the words come.

"President Bush was correct that weapons of mass destruction pose a threat to the world, but in a world where weapons of mass destruction are proliferating, peace is the only pragmatic option. It is war now that is naïve." I paused. "Your Honor, during this hearing I've been looking at the Seal of the United States on the wall behind you, and the question that keeps haunting me is: Whatever happened to the olive branch?"

The hearing was a formality. We all knew that the

decision had already been made and nothing we said would change the outcome.

After the hearing, we were instructed to report to the parole office.

My parole officer, a young African American woman who had pictures of Malcolm X, Martin Luther King, Jr., and a rather abstract painting of a Black church service on her wall, asked me the intake questions.

"When you entered your plea, were you asked to assist the US government in any way?"

I laughed. "No, but I would be willing to, if they'd like some advice."

She smiled.

After the paperwork was completed and they had taken our photographs and fingerprints, we were sent home until further notice.

A week later, on a sunny spring morning, Earth Day, the "self-surrenders"—as the prison staff would call us—and some of our supporters gathered in front of the Federal Building once more to share prayers and a ritual of anointing. Then we walked together toward the detention center a block away, singing, "Gonna lay down my sword and shield down by the riverside."

When we reached the detention center, the nine of us—six women and three men—entered the lobby. On the wall, George W. Bush and John Ashcroft smiled from their picture frames; all around us, uniformed guards, just about to begin their shifts, stood around finishing their morning coffee. I felt like I had stepped into the thick of the Emperor's dream.

During several hours of intake we were strip-searched twice and given our maximum security prison clothes—orange jumpsuit, orange underwear, orange bra, orange socks, orange T-shirt, orange Keds. Then, a male guard escorted me, my wrists handcuffed behind my back, down a long corridor to my cell, the jangle of the keys hanging from his belt reverberating against the bare cinder block walls. Other women prisoners watched from behind the narrow windows in their cell doors as we passed.

We got to the last cell on the corridor and the guard unlocked the door. Inside, one of my fellow protesters—Janeal, a tall, gray-haired woman in her sixties who lived with her husband in a Quaker community just outside Philadelphia—was waiting for me.

The guard locked the door behind me and told me to back up and stoop down so he could remove my handcuffs through a small slot in the door. Then the echo of footfalls and jangling keys receded back down the corridor.

We were held in the SHU, the Special Housing Unit reserved for problem prisoners, who were often kept in solitary confinement. There we would be kept in lock-down, confined to our cells twenty-four hours a day, except for an hour of exercise Monday through Friday.

Our cell—twelve feet long and ten feet wide—contained a steel bunk bed with thin mattresses (orange linens provided), a metal table with attached stools bolted to the wall, a metal shower stall, a steel toilet, a small steel sink with a piece of sheet metal above it for a mirror, and a suicide-prevention hook for towels—designed to release if too much weight were hung from it. On the far wall was a narrow window of frosted glass. There was no clock, but judging by the lack of light coming through the frosted window I knew it must be late evening.

I looked at Janeal. "I'd like to bless the space."

"What a great idea!" She thought for a moment. "I know! We could use the blessing my family used to say over meals when I was growing up. We can just change some of the words."

As she spoke the blessing I wrote it down on a piece of toilet paper, using the small ball point pen they had given me during intake. When we were done, I taped the toilet paper to the wall with a small bit of Scotch tape that had been left there.

Spirit, we thank thee for this cell
Thy bounteous love provides.
Stay with us here that ours may be
A cell where peace abides.

Let all our words be soft with love,
Our thoughts all free from shame.
Let every act beneath this roof
Be worthy of thy name.

Janeal discovered that the words could be sung to the tune of "Our God, Our Help in Ages Past," and from then on we sang it over each meal.

Like me, Janeal liked to sing. She was an alto and she'd been praying for a cellmate who was a soprano, which I am. We had both grown up Presbyterian and knew many of the same hymns; on that first day we sang them in two-part harmony, delighting in the acoustics of our cell.

After lights-out, we spent a chilly night beneath our thin orange blankets. Several times during the night the guard making the nightly rounds shined a flashlight into our cell to check on us.

The next morning we were greeted by the sound of Bernadette, another woman in our group, singing from her cell down the corridor.

"Good morning, good morning! We're all in our places, with sunshiny faces!"

Janeal and I had our morning prayer time and then I taught her a couple of songs. Once she'd mastered them, we called them out to our companions down the corridor. They joined in and I accompanied us with percussion, using one of our metal stools as a drum.

Soon, the slots in the doors down the cellblock were clanging open with breakfast.

Later that day I received a visit from volunteers from a prisoner visitation and support organization. The guard led me, handcuffed, down the corridor toward the visitation room.

Across from the guards' station I saw a man in one of the holding rooms. His face was bloodied, and the holding room window that looked out onto the corridor was streaked with blood. As we approached he looked at me with haunted, wild eyes. At first I thought he'd been beaten, but I overheard the guards talking to one another.

"Did you see that? He just keeps pounding his head against the glass!"

"I know. He's crazy."

Looking into the crazed eyes of that man I knew I was looking into the madness of an insane idea that had manifested itself here in concrete walls and locked doors. The illusion of separateness that originated in the mind had taken on form—walls isolating people, just as the ego does, from one another, from the Earth. Humanity, like this crazed man, was bloodying itself against its mind's own illusion, not knowing that it was resistance itself that gave the walls solidity.

Earlier in the day I had stood with my eye glued to a tiny pinprick of clear glass I had discovered on the frosted window of our cell. Smaller than the head of a pin, it was my only view to the outside world. Looking through it I could make out the basic outlines of buildings, cars, a distant highway. I realized that for me the cruelest aspect of imprisonment would be to live months and even years never seeing a moonrise or a flower opening to the sun, never feeling the breeze on my skin or breathing in the smell of the woods after a rain, never hearing birdsong or touching the rough bark of a tree or walking a beach and feeling the sand beneath my feet. Ripping people away from the web of life and caging them in a world of artificial lights and unyielding surfaces was inhumane, the antithesis of the spiritual truth of interconnection. I could understand why someone would beat his head against the walls until he bled.

We weren't given our allotted hour of exercise time on Friday, but at least Janeal and I received a few items we'd requested—cups, shampoo, and a few sheets of paper—and we were finally permitted our phone calls. The counselor came to get me, handcuffed me, and took me to one of the holding rooms, then wheeled a phone in on a metal cart.

"What number do you want me to dial?" he asked gruffly.

I gave him the number and got Kip's voicemail.

"Hi honey. It's me. I just want you to know that I'm okay. My cellmate, Janeal, and I are getting along really well. I hope everything's okay with you. Let me give you my prisoner number so you can pass it along. If anybody wants to send me mail, they'll need it. I'm thinking about you. I love you very much!"

I hung up the receiver and the counselor escorted me back to my cell.

That afternoon a guard came to our door.

"Pearce, you have a visitor."

He handcuffed me and led me to the visitation booth. When he opened the door I saw Susan sitting on the other side of the Plexiglas partition. We had been hoping that as a clergyperson, she would be allowed to visit me.

I noticed the shock in her eyes when she saw me in handcuffs, wearing an orange jumpsuit, and escorted by the very large guard. After he removed the cuffs I went over and sat down at the counter. We each picked up the phone handset on the wall.

"How are you doing?" she asked.

"I'm okay. It's pretty surreal though. How are things with you?"

"Pretty good. Everybody sends their love."

"Thank you. Please give them my love as well."

"I will. Say, I had an amazing dream the other night. Would you like to hear it?"

"Of course!"

"Okay. So in the dream I'm on my way to visit you but I get lost. I wander around and around, but I can't find the prison. Finally, I end up in the woods, in the place where you had your energy opening. But in the dream it has a stream flowing around it where dolphins and whales are swimming, and little children are running around and playing."

"What an incredible dream!"

"I know! It felt so beautiful, and hopeful."

We visited for a while longer. When it was time for Susan to leave we placed our hands against the Plexiglas partition, looking one another in the eye as the energy flowed between us.

Later I journaled about Susan's dream.

Such a beautiful image . . . To know that I am in that space . . . outside the artificial barriers of time and space. And that I'm encircled by dolphins, whales, children. The punishment [of prison] truly becomes illusory if there's no time and no space. This entire institution is built upon the false concept of separateness. These walls are meant to heighten one's sense of separateness, which is the ego's paradigm. But what if one relinquishes the ego identification and its illusions of separateness? Then incarceration loses its capacity to inflict suffering. If I know that here with me are the woods and the dolphins and the whales and the elephants and my loved ones . . . If I know that there is no time but only eternity—only Being. This entire system is the manifestation of the egoic worldview—which is a false worldview.

A couple of days before reporting to the detention center to serve my sentence, I had a Reiki session with Zoana. Afterward she shared an instruction she had intuitively heard.

"One thing I was getting was that you should ask your friends to check in with you at four o'clock in the afternoon while you're in prison." She laughed at the seemingly bizarre information. "What does that mean, 'check in'? How can they 'check in' with you when you're in jail?!" She laughed again. Then her face turned serious and she closed her eyes to listen inwardly. After a moment she opened her eyes again. "Ask them to meditate with you—at four o'clock. Every day." She tossed her head back and laughed some more.

I had followed the advice I'd been given. Once I got to the prison, though, and saw that there was no clock in our cell and no way of knowing the time of day, I was disappointed. I had been looking forward to "checking in" with my friends from inside the walls. Now there would be no way to synchronize my meditation time with theirs.

But on my first day in prison, I found out that four o'clock was when the guards did the daily head count. Precisely at four an alarm went off throughout the prison, and all the prisoners were supposed to stand in the middle of their cells until the guards came down the corridor to count us. Four o'clock, as it turned out, was the only time of day when I knew what time of day it was.

Each afternoon when the alarm sounded, rather than stand in the middle of our cell I took my seat on the top bunk, crossed my legs, and began meditating. When the guards came by, Janeal told them I was meditating, and they never disturbed me. It was my small act of peaceful noncompliance.

Janeal was a joy to be with. I couldn't have asked for a better cellmate. She was considerate, playful, kind, and funny. Besides music, we shared an interest in arts and crafts. Every couple of days a volunteer would come down the corridor wheeling a cart loaded with magazines and books and Janeal and I would take a couple of magazines to use for collages. We tore out pictures and words and pasted them together with dabs of toothpaste. As the toothpaste on my collages dried, it bled through the paper and, in keeping with the color scheme of the SHU, turned orange.

Janeal also showed me how to make origami boxes with folded sheets of paper, in which we stashed the numerous packets delivered with each meal: sugar, instant coffee, and a powdered orange-flavored drink called "Outrageous Orange."

She also tore out letters and pasted a message on the end of our bunk bed frame so it would be visible from the door: God Bless the Whole World—No Exceptions. In her spare time Janeal recorded every detail of our experience for the booklet her Quaker community, Pendle Hill, would publish: *A Good Week Behind Bars*.

We had some meaningful conversations with the guards as they made their rounds, some of whom were very respectful and had their own misgivings about the war.

One of them stopped outside our door.

"Why are you here?" she asked.

"We were protesting the war," I said.

"But why?"

"Because we thought it was wrong and would only cause more violence."

"Here too?"

"Yes, here too."

Another of the guards told us about his brother who had been in Iraq and had brought back videos.

"It's more horrible than you can imagine," he said.

On Monday they finally let us have our hour of exercise. Unfortunately, I was experiencing vertigo, so I stayed behind, but I could hear the others singing from the exercise "cage" down the hall—"Amazing Grace," "Those Who Believe in Freedom Cannot Rest Until It Comes," "Halle Halle," "Michael Row the Boat Ashore," "Gonna Lay Down My Sword and Shield," and more. I stood with my ear to the door, weeping at the beauty of their singing reverberating throughout the cellblock.

On Tuesday, feeling better, I joined the others for our exercise time, singing songs and doing circle dances. That evening, Janeal and I waited and waited for our mail to be delivered.

When one of the guards came by on his rounds, Janeal called out, "Excuse me, sir. Do you know why we haven't received our mail yet?"

"Because somebody got so much that it's taking them a long time to open it all and inspect it."

That somebody turned out to be me. A couple of hours later he delivered a stack of mail so large it barely fit through the door slot—mail from friends and family, but mostly from people at Tab. I was overwhelmed by their outpouring of support.

Mail wasn't the only way I was experiencing the congregation's support, either. Many of them had made pledges to engage in jail solidarity, doing things or relinquishing things throughout the course of the week to keep me and the other prisoners in the forefront of their minds. They had also set up a prayer rotation to hold me in prayer, and all week I could feel its effects—an energy of love was buoying me up. On Tuesday some of them joined me for a pre-arranged day of fasting.

All week long Janeal and I had tried to be a presence of peace in the prison, treating those we encountered with respect, practicing compassion, not stereotyping others just because of their role in the system. We were attempting to bring a different sort of energy into that place. On the last day before our release, I had a vision while in prayer of the walls of the detention center cracking.

Wednesday had already arrived, the day of our release, and anticipating further strip searches I made a paste out of some of the Outrageous Orange powder drink; there were three words I wanted Janeal to paint on my back. She had her misgivings and needed a bit of coaxing, but finally she agreed.

I drew down the top of my jumpsuit and turned my bare back toward her. Slowly and deliberately, tracing each letter down my spine, she wrote the words with her finger.

Feeling the cool paste drawn across my skin, I felt I was engaging in a ritual. I was acknowledging that peace requires vulnerability, laying aside all the ego's protective shields—becoming, as the prison staff had called us, self-surrenders.

When Janeal was done, the three words I had requested were emblazoned on my back in bold orange letters:

STRIP
FOR
PEACE

When it was time to go, we tucked our collages among our mail so we could smuggle them out, leaving behind the message "God Bless the Whole World—No Exceptions" pasted to the bed frame and the piece of toilet paper with the blessing taped to the wall. The guards led us to the waiting area, where we were reunited with the rest of our group. While waiting in the corridor, I noticed a piece of paper Bernadette had tucked under her arm. In bold letters it said, "No One Wins."

While we waited to be processed for release there was one last delivery of mail. As an expression of thanks for our witness, one of the local Quaker Meetings had sent cards for all of us, each with a different animal on the front. On mine was a drawing of an elephant.

When we got to the storage room where our own clothes were returned to us, I was disappointed that we weren't strip-searched again. So Janeal and I showed the female guard standing nearby the message on my back. She laughed.

Now that all six of us were together again in a holding cell, awaiting our final release, we all had a chance to sing together one last time. The acoustics were phenomenal.

Soon a guard came over and opened the slot in the door so they could hear us better from the guards' station. Then another came over and asked, "Are you-all a choir?"

Bernadette answered, "Yes. We used to call ourselves the Prisoners of Conscience Choir, but now we call ourselves the Outrageous Orange Sextet."

Finally we were led to the elevator, taken to the basement, and quietly released out a back door. Stepping into the bright sunshine of a chilly spring day, we found our loved ones and supporters waiting for us. One of them had brought a loaf of bread, which he asked me to bless. We broke and shared it, hugged each other, then said our good-byes and went our way.

Chapter 22: Weary Spires

"So how much do you think it will cost us?" I asked.

I and a couple Tab members were meeting with a trustee from the Presbytery to talk about some needed repairs to one of Tabernacle's spires. Some of the stones were in danger of falling, and just a few weeks earlier the massive stone tower of a church of the same vintage just six blocks away had collapsed into a mountain of rubble. Fortunately no one had been injured, but it had brought home to us the seriousness of the situation.

Tabernacle was an architectural gem. With its gargoyles, iconography, and texts carved into the stones, and the three large stone angels protruding from the corners of its bell tower, it had been hailed as one of the premier examples of neo-Gothic architecture in the country when it was first built in the late 1800s. It wasn't surprising that after more than a century the elaborate structure needed repair.

It was a familiar story. So many congregations were saddled with aging buildings that had once supported their worship life and mission, but with dwindling memberships the stately old buildings had become sinkholes, devouring precious resources. In an ironic role reversal, many congregations seemed to exist in order to support their buildings rather than the other way around.

Tabernacle, sitting on prime real estate next to the University of Pennsylvania, was in a very different situation. While not an affluent church, we had a steady stream of rental income and enough of a reserve fund to cover the costs of repair.

But the situation seemed symbolic to me of all the resources and energy that went into bolstering the Church of the past—not just its buildings but its beliefs.

What would happen if we just let the crumbling structures and archaic doctrines fall, rather than continually defending them and propping them up? What sort of resurrection might the Church experience if it let itself die, and what might its new architecture look like?

I was fairly certain it wouldn't be reaching up to the heavens with lofty steeples. It would most likely be close to the Earth, and round, conveying the understanding that divinity is incarnated in everything. Rather than the cross, its central symbol might be the tree: the cross itself resurrected.

I was reminded of Salisbury Cathedral and how its soaring spire told the story of humans trying to reach a God in the heavens rather than encountering the sacred on Earth. Perhaps the stones in our spires were telling us they were tired of being up in the sky, that they wanted to return to the Earth where they belonged.

I understood why so many people resisted letting the old beliefs die. It was painful and frightening. Just a few days after my release from prison, I had attended a seminar led by theologian Walter Wink called *Jesus' Way of Healing*. Walter talked about what he called the Integrated Worldview, referring to many of the principles of quantum physics that

I had found so compelling, and how the belief in separation between heaven and earth, spirit and matter, was outmoded.

Our discussions were stimulating, and I was excited to explore these concepts in the company of others. But I noticed that as soon as we turned to Bible study we reverted back to using the same old language of separation that permeated the scriptures. God was still spoken of as a spiritual entity distinct from us and all creation.

Finally I posed the question we all seemed to be skirting: "What do we mean by 'God' if all is one, and we are included?"

No sooner were the words out of my mouth than another pastor, distressed, said to Walter, "Please tell me there is still a Holy Other God! I don't want to give that up!"

Seeing his fear at the possibility of "losing" God, I realized how terrifying this leap could be. I sensed that at the root of his panic was the ego's deep fear of loneliness and isolation. The ego is not able to comprehend or imagine the experience of indivisible Oneness, because that is a Reality it cannot enter. The two go hand in hand: union with the All also means the death of the ego.

It also means the death of our powerlessness. An external God allows us to project all divinity and power outside ourselves. Seeing God as the parental, omnipotent Other allows us to see ourselves as passive and dependent—mere recipients rather than active co-creators with Life.

The disconnect I was experiencing in the seminar between the emerging worldview and traditional Christian beliefs was the same one I experienced every week in worship. No matter what I might say in a sermon about the integrated worldview, the hymns, liturgies, and scriptures—even the ways we prayed—reinforced a worldview of separation.

Perhaps these two worlds simply could not be held together. And trying to do so was beginning to take its toll on me. I was growing increasingly aware of the energy I was expending trying to work within a theological architecture that no longer held true for me. Like the spires, I was growing weary.

A memory came back to me of a morning when I was a child attending Vacation Bible School. We were outside in front of the church reciting our pledges to the Bible and the Christian flag. It was a bright summer morning, and I happened to look up at the belfry towering above us. Clouds were gliding swiftly across the blue sky, creating the impression that the red sandstone tower was toppling. I pointed it out to my friend standing next to me, and we decided to play a practical joke on Agnes, the church administrator, who was standing behind us.

We turned to her, pointed up to the tower, and whispered, "Agnes! The steeple is falling!"

She looked up and her face went ashen, no doubt imagining the impending catastrophe: dozens of children crushed to death beneath red sandstone debris.

All these years later I didn't know why that particular moment had lingered with me, but I thought perhaps it was because that morning, when I was a child, I looked up at the sky and I really *did* see the church falling—and the sight shook me to my core.

Chapter 23: Dark Night of the Soul

Winter 2006. I was back at Ghost Ranch, sitting next to the labyrinth. I didn't have the energy to walk it.

It had been three and a half years since my opening in the woods. In the tumultuous years since, I had frequently assailed myself for my inability to consistently stay awake to the unified Reality I had seen. As the time for my annual retreat approached I sank into deep self-loathing. I had no willpower left, and everything I had ever thought I knew was being stripped away from within. I was in a void, a nothingness, a spiritual nadir. There was only one thing I knew with certainty: my mother loved me. But even this gave me no consolation. It was simply information.

I sensed I was undergoing a cleansing of a profound nature. I never wanted to have to go through this painful experience again. My only prayer was, "Make the darkness complete."

After sitting next to the labyrinth for hours, tears pooling in my eyes for no apparent reason, I decided to go back to my room to lie down.

I fell into a sort of stasis. I was still conscious yet I felt inwardly paralyzed, my body seemingly incapable of moving. This went on for perhaps an hour.

Gradually it lifted, and my ability and my will to move returned, but something remarkable had happened.

Despite all of the spiritual breakthroughs I had experienced in recent years, I had felt a deep loneliness within me all my life. It was as though in the core of my being there was an emptiness that could never be filled.

When the stasis lifted, that emptiness was gone. All loneliness was gone. The dark night had done its work.

Chapter 24: Stranger in a Strange Land

I am in Israel traveling with an interfaith group. We are in Jerusalem, near the Western Wall of the Temple, and Shabbat is just about to begin. In the waning sunlight people are pouring into the plaza. Orthodox men in black, *payot* dangling from beneath their fur hats, women in Israeli Defense Force uniforms, yeshiva students dancing and singing, snaking their way through the sea of people, headed for the Wall. Their joy is palpable. After centuries of Diaspora they have come home.

As the yeshiva students dance past me, I feel the earth beneath my feet tremble to the beat of their dance; their song pounds against my chest like a drum, and I am jolted by a sudden, troubling realization: I don't belong here. Not just in this place, but in this tradition.

Jesus is sitting on a hillside in the Galilee teaching, surrounded by a crowd of people. He is wearing a *tallit*, and I see now that everyone else is wearing one too.

He is speaking a language I don't understand, but it is obvious he is talking about things that are of concern to the people here. They listen in rapt attention.

I'm confused, and disoriented. I don't know how I got here, so far from home. This is not my land, the desert God is not my God.

I ask a man sitting nearby if he can tell me where the stone circles and sacred groves are, but he doesn't understand what I'm saying. I walk off into the desert, not knowing where to go.

I am about to take a trip to Israel and I have a dream. All it says is: "Listen to *ha'erets*." Listen to the land.

Now I'm in the Church of the Holy Sepulcher, where Jesus is said to have been crucified. I'm trying to excavate through the floor of the church to find the land beneath it. I know it can tell me what really happened. But there is too much gold ornamentation and too many religious mosaics in the way. No matter how deep I dig I can't get past them.

A Patriarch is off to the side, looking at me disapprovingly. Then I remember, this is the section of the church reserved for the Greek Orthodox.

I'm sitting next to the Jordan River. Our tour bus has stopped here so that the Christians in our group can reaffirm their baptisms. I choose not to participate. Upstream the others emerge from the tourist shop wearing the white gowns they have rented. They are standing in a circle in the river praying together, preparing to baptize one another.

I dangle my hand in the water, then cup my palm to draw a handful of water up. I gaze at it and it shows me something.

It shows me how it has traveled for millions of years across the face of the Earth, flowing through every stream and every ocean. I see how for eons it has traveled across the sky, fallen as rain, crystallized into icebergs and glaciers, coursed through the veins of billions upon billions of creatures. In this moment it happens to be flowing through a particular riverbed known as the Jordan.

I understand what it is telling me: It is no more sacred here than it is anywhere else. All rivers are equally holy.

I'm in the television room in my dormitory in Germany, sitting with German students watching the mini-series *Holocaust*. It is the first time there has been any public discourse about what happened to the Jews during the Third Reich.

After the show I return to my room and turn on my radio. There is a talk show on. People are calling in to air their feelings after the telecast. A woman is on the phone talking about watching her Jewish neighbors being taken away. She is sobbing. "*Warum habe ich nichts gemacht? Warum habe ich nichts gemacht?*" Why didn't I do anything?

Now I'm crossing through the Wall at Checkpoint Charlie into East Berlin. One of the other exchange students has strapped an art book to his leg under his jeans to smuggle it across to a friend. The Soviet soldier doesn't notice the bulge and waves him through.

I'm on the other side of the Wall now, driving through Bethlehem. Begging children and adult men peddling cheap trinkets run alongside our bus. They have a look of desperation in their eyes. We drive past them, past the dilapidated buildings, on our way to the Church of the Nativity.

No hope. No hope. No hope.

Palestinians and Jews are chanting together, a Greek chorus:

No hope. No hope. No hope.

The chant becomes an antiphon:

This conflict cannot be resolved.
This land is too small for two states.
One state isn't possible.
The divorce has already happened.
The damage is irreparable.
We're past the peace process.
No hope. No hope. No hope.

I'm with a group having lunch with an Israeli who lives in one of the settlements in the West Bank. As she speaks I am amazed by her certainty and conviction that what she and her family are doing is right, reclaiming the land God had given them, even though the settlements are eroding all possibilities for the Palestinians to have a land of their own.

I see something protruding from her ear. At first it looks like a small Torah scroll, but then I can see it is the roster from a concentration camp. It has made her unable to hear.

Outside the restaurant I hear the sound of bulldozers. I look out the window and see them uprooting ancient olive trees. A family of Palestinians is standing nearby, wailing. I'm in tenth grade, learning how to write a research paper. My English teacher tells us we need to choose a topic. I want to research the thing I have never been able to understand, the one thing that has haunted me from my youth: the Holocaust. But the topic is too big. I have to narrow it down. I decide I will write a paper on Adolf Eichmann.

I'm walking through Yad Vashem, the museum in Jerusalem dedicated to the Jews who were killed in the Holocaust. Room after room of artifacts, videos, and photographs tell the story of the atrocity. I stop in front of one of the cases. There is a black-and-white photograph of a group of people lined up next to the train tracks, having just arrived in Auschwitz. One woman stands out. She is wearing a wool coat and holds a small cardboard suitcase in her hand. She is looking directly at me.

Now I'm outside the museum, in the Avenue of the Righteous—the memorial to the gentiles who risked their lives to help Jews escape the Nazis. I am looking at the engraved names, wondering if I will come upon my own.

Now I'm sitting in the courtyard outside the cafeteria having lunch with a Jewish woman in our group. She asks me, "What does Christianity teach about forgiveness?"

I know it is a loaded question, and I hesitate to answer. I begin by saying I have no place speaking about forgiveness in relation to the suffering inflicted during the Holocaust. All I can do is share my own understanding, that forgiveness is a way to take back our power, and that we don't have to wait for the wrongdoer to repent. Leaving it in the hands of the wrongdoer to decide if forgiveness will happen is to remain forever imprisoned in suffering and injustice.

"It is the only way to set the future free."

She looks at me and nods.

I'm back at the Western Wall as Shabbat is beginning. I have written a prayer on a scrap of paper that I'm holding in my hand. It is my prayer for humanity: "Transform story."

I join the jostling throng of people, inching my way forward, heading for the section of the Wall that is cordoned off for the women. It is half the size of the section reserved for the men and we crowd together shoulder to shoulder.

Finally I reach the Wall, and I struggle to find an open space large enough between the massive stones for my prayer. Every crack, for as high as I can reach, is filled with wadded scraps of paper.

There is a woman wearing a headscarf to my left, and as I clumsily try to stuff my paper between the stones she looks over at me disapprovingly. I finally manage to wedge my paper in among the others and withdraw.

I'm standing with a group on the shore of the Sea of Galilee at sunrise. The sky is beginning to glow orange. Hundreds of birds are flying above the water. Jesus is here. He is talking about a reality he calls the Realm of God. He is telling us to look at the birds of the air and at the reeds undulating in the lapping water. They are our teachers.

Now he is walking off toward a hill to pray, alone.

A legion of centurions has appeared, marching over the hill. They are wearing helmets and metal breastplates, carrying spears and swords. I know when they arrive there will be a cataclysm of unimaginable proportions. The land will be devastated, the people will be slaughtered, the lake will turn red with blood.

I know that Jesus knows the escape route. He tried explaining it to me once, but I couldn't understand.

I cry out to him, "Empire will kill us!"

I know he hears me, but he doesn't stop. I can see now that he is carrying a cross, walking directly toward the oncoming legion.

Chapter 25: The Last Outpost

Sitting in Tabernacle's Fellowship Room, the congregation was circled around me and we were laughing uproariously. They were throwing a party for my tenth anniversary as their pastor and they had just given me a gift: a clergy shirt, with a card that said, "Proper clergy attire—for your next arrest!"

It had been several months now since my unsettling trip to Israel, a journey I had never planned to take until I received an invitation from the Jewish Community Relations Council of Philadelphia to participate in an all-expenses-paid, interfaith trip. I had no idea the experience would only distance me further from the religion of my upbringing.

While I was in Israel I felt as though I were in a dream. The past and present intermingled, and I was overwhelmed by the confusing kaleidoscope of history I found myself in. How had I, a North American woman of European and British descent, become an adherent to a religion that arose in a desert of the distant Middle East?

Obviously I knew the historical answer: Christianity was adopted by the Roman Empire, imperial Christianity spread into Europe and England, and from there to North America. Like an invasive species, it overran the indigenous spiritualities it encountered.

While in Israel I was acutely aware of a message I had received on one of my visits to Ghost Ranch while walking the labyrinth, delivered with the characteristic impartial calmness, free of any fanfare: "Release all concept of enemy." The message went on to say, "There are no enemies. There are only those who do not know who they are."

That message helped unlock for me a new meaning in the dream of the powerful woman I had had so many years before: "Soon you will 'no' no one." To "no" someone was to negate their very right to exist. Israel seemed a land held hostage to the concept of enemy, of "no-ing" the other.

As a result of my trip to Israel two things happened. On the one hand, I felt more drawn than ever to Jesus's teachings. I believed there was something at the heart of what he understood and was doing that our planet needed more urgently than ever. I was well aware that the current strife between the Jews and Palestinians was the direct legacy of the Roman Empire of Jesus's day. When the Jews revolted against Rome, just forty years after Jesus was crucified, Rome destroyed Jerusalem, including the Temple, and the Jews were driven into exile. They wouldn't return for almost 2,000 years, after the catastrophe of the Holocaust. And when they did, the Palestinians lost their homeland just as the Jews had. It seemed to me Jesus had been offering another way to deal with empire, something much more radical than violent revolt.

But even though I hungered to understand Jesus's teachings more fully, my visit to Israel left me feeling more alienated from Jesus himself. While many of the Christians in our group felt like they had come home, I was feeling like a stranger in a strange land, wandering through a culture that wasn't mine, surrounded by a language that wasn't mine, in a land that felt foreign.

In my previous travels I had visited other unfamiliar geographies, but this time it was different. I had come to believe there is a strong link between a particular land and the spiritual sensibilities that have arisen among the people who inhabit it. Just as the terroir of a specific vineyard endows its wine with unique characteristics, the Middle Eastern desert created, in a sense, a different sort of God than the British Isles and European countrysides of my ancestors.

Before my trip I had felt disenfranchised from much of Christianity because its doctrines no longer coincided with what I had experienced in my own life. But now the feeling of alienation went even deeper. Jesus seemed like a complete foreigner to me. He was a Jew who lived as a Jew, practiced as a Jew, walked the countryside of his Jewish ancestors, and spoke to the concerns of his own people, the Jews. Even the concept of Messiah was Jewish—so who was I to enter the fray of that ancient argument?

I didn't know what my heritage was anymore. The pre-Christian spirituality of the British Isles of my ancestors had been lost. The spirituality of the place where I currently lived—Lenapehoking, as Eastern Pennsylvania was known before the arrival of the Europeans—didn't belong to me. I had become a spiritual nomad.

At least I still had Tab. We had been together for ten years now, and in many ways it felt like the honeymoon had never ended. Despite all of my questions about my relationship with Christianity, this was a place that continued to feel like home. The people of Tabernacle had been so supportive, standing with me in my activist involvements, sharing my passion for the environment, welcoming my theological explorations. Although I was a closeted mystic—not speaking about what was going on in my spiritual life except with my closest friends—I could share with the congregation the perspectives my experiences had led me to. When I gave a sermon series titled *Quantum Christianity*, in which I explored the ways in which the discoveries of quantum physics aligned with what I now believed was at the heart of Jesus's message, the congregation had responded enthusiastically.

Tab was a refuge, a sanctuary, the last outpost at the edge of the Church. I knew I would never find another congregation like it, nor would I ever try.

Chapter 26: Jesus the Shaman

There was one spiritual orientation that seemed to coincide with what had been happening in my spiritual life: shamanism. Found in every part of the world and every culture, shamanism saw all things as interconnected, understood the Earth as sacred, comprehended that we are living in a dream and can effect change in the manifested world by interacting with the invisible realm with our consciousness and the seeds of our intention. It was a spiritual orientation I wanted to explore.

In the summer of 2008 I attended a seminar at Omega Institute led by author and shamanic practitioner John Perkins. I had been very interested in John's work ever since one of his books, *Confessions of an Economic Hit Man,* showed up in my mailbox, sent to me by his publisher unrequested.

John was exposing the collective dream. Like Toto in the Wizard of Oz, he was pulling back the curtain on our illusion and unmasking the devastating mechanisms of empire. When I saw in the bibliography of *Confessions* that he had also written a book titled *The World Is As You Dream It,* I knew I had stumbled upon a kindred spirit.

Like myself, John had been a Peace Corps Volunteer in Ecuador, though more than two decades before me. While he was there he had apprenticed with a shaman in the Amazonian village where he lived. One day during the seminar, as we sat together on the dining porch eating lunch, I told him that I was a pastor and had also been a Peace Corps Volunteer in Ecuador, and I filled him in about some of my recent experiences.

"You know," John said, "there's a Quichua shaman I know. He lives not far from where you did your training, in fact. When you walk inside his house there's a big picture of Jesus on the wall. I knew he wasn't Christian, so I asked him why he had a picture of Jesus. He said, 'Because Jesus was a very powerful shaman.'"

Chills went down my spine. I realized this is what I wanted to understand: the shamanism of Jesus. Whatever it was he had been doing went beyond individual healing. He had engaged the underpinnings of imperial reality with a different consciousness, a shamanic consciousness.

The seminar John was leading was about shapeshifting, and I was keenly aware of how Christianity had undergone a dramatic shapeshift since its beginnings. Jesus, who had embodied the antithesis of imperial consciousness, had become the sacred mascot of the empire after the Roman Emperor Constantine converted to Christianity. The whole belief system had become an expression of the very ego-empire consciousness that had dissolved in Jesus's mind and from which he had sought to free others. I wondered whether it was possible for Christianity to shapeshift once again.

During the seminar we participated in shamanic journeying using drumming—a common practice among indigenous people—as a vehicle to dissolve ego consciousness and experience a different dimension. One such journey was particularly meaningful to me:

I am in a mountain meadow and see many of my friends approaching. When we all come together we start doing a circle dance, and a beam of Light begins to descend from the sky. We dance around the beam and then move inside it, dancing our dance inside the Light.

A being descends down through the beam of Light and comes toward me. It is Jesus, who then shapeshifts into an old woman I encountered in a previous journey. In that journey She gave me a shaman's drum. I see both faces as one face, and I know that they are one and the same. The being looks deeply into my eyes. His eyes are black, and in each iris is a spiral galaxy. She asks me if I will bring peace, harmony, and compassion into the world. I ponder the question, feeling its significance. I say yes.

She offers me a robe of shimmering light that flows continually into different undulating colors. He puts the robe on me and it merges with me, becomes me. Then She gives me another gift, a snake of Light coiled around her arm that becomes a flame of white Light constantly shapeshifting into many forms. He places this gift in me as well. I sense it is an energy that can take on any form needed in any given moment or situation.

Then the Light Being ascends up the column of Light, and I return to this world.

Chapter 27: Constantine's Vision

The moment I entered the gallery in the art museum my consciousness was altered, and I could see that the medieval armor on display told the story of humanity's ego, this long dream of suffering in which we have perceived ourselves to be separate, have tried to shield ourselves from death, have battled with those we perceive as enemies.

Looking at one of the pieces—its breastplate adorned with an engraving of the crucifixion—I thought about Constantine's conversion, which precipitated Christianity's shapeshift into an imperial, warfaring religion.

I knew the legend of his conversion—that on the eve of battle he had a vision of a cross in the sky and a voice telling him, "By this you will conquer." The next day he went into battle bearing the insignia of the cross, won the battle, and became a believer.

But I had always been skeptical of Constantine's conversion, especially the part about a spiritual presence coming to his aid to vanquish his enemies. That didn't sound like any presence even remotely associated with the Jesus I knew. For years I had wondered if perhaps Constantine's conversion had been a ploy to usurp the Jesus movement that was spreading quickly through the Roman world, unleashing all sorts of anti-imperial, egalitarian beliefs and practices.

Whether or not his conversion was authentic, Constantine left a lasting mark on the religion. He was the one who convened the first Church council, ordering the bishops to create a creed that would homogenize Christian belief. With the emperor's input, they finally succeeded in writing the Nicene Creed. Orthodoxy was born and all other strands of Christian interpretation were condemned as heresy. Of course, the fact that there *were* bishops to convene indicated how much the Church had already begun to abandon Jesus's radically egalitarian teachings. Ego had already made great inroads into the religion, though they were nothing like what would happen when empire got a hold of it.

Now, as I gazed at the armor in the glass case before me—a silent, ghostly sentry from the past—I began to question my own skepticism about Constantine's vision. I had had enough mystical experiences myself by now that it seemed perfectly plausible to me that he had seen and heard something. But if that were the case, how could it possibly be that Jesus—if it had been Jesus—had come to him to suggest battle tactics? I mean, really. Jesus was hardly about aiding and abetting empire.

That's when it dawned on me. "He misinterpreted the vision!" I whispered to myself.

Jesus's own disciples hadn't been able to understand what he was trying to convey. How could Constantine—so thoroughly immersed in the ego's world and consumed by its drive for power—ever hope to?

If Constantine *did* see a vision of the cross, he must not have understood what it meant. He would have seen it through the lens of ego, as a symbol of conquest over his enemies. The cross's function, after all, from his imperial perspective, was to terrorize and subjugate. He would have been clueless to the fact that Jesus had shapeshifted the cross from a tool of torture and domination into a demonstration of the unreality of death, the illusory nature of the ego, and the powerlessness of the world's empires.

If Constantine actually did have a vision, it wouldn't have come to ensure his victory over his "enemies." It would have come to show him a way out of the egoic insanity consuming him.

Perhaps, I realized, Constantine really *did* have a mystical experience, but he interpreted it in the only way he knew how: from the perspective of the ego and its imperialistic drives. And the rest was, literally, history.

Chapter 28: Circling Back

I was sitting alone beside the pool in the canyon where we had scattered Tricia's ashes eight years earlier. Watching the water bugs' shadows darting across the rocky bottom, I reflected on how deeply Tricia's life had touched my own. I don't know what I would have done without her in seminary when spiritual earthquakes left my faith in rubble. I thought about her courageous struggle with her disease, and I remembered the cherished moments when I had felt her presence even after she died.

I had returned to California to make a pilgrimage to the places that had been significant to her: her home; her alma mater, Stanford, and its hospital, where she died; the church in Palo Alto she had belonged to; and this beloved canyon.

Now time seemed to be doubling back on itself as I sat in the place where we had scattered her ashes.

Opposite me, water flowed over polished boulders covered with moss and yellow bay leaves, tumbling into the deep pool for a momentary pause before continuing its journey down the canyon. A presence seemed to be all around me—in the water, the trees, the rocks, the dragonflies and hummingbirds that flitted by. I sensed Tricia's spirit diffused into this living oneness.

I pulled my tin whistle out of my backpack and began to play, the music echoing against the rock outcroppings. The sound of it unlocked my heart. Grief that had been locked up for eight years poured forth.

When the cleansing tears finally ceased, I could feel that something inside had shifted. The past was past.

As the sun began to descend into late afternoon, I started back down the canyon.

Kip flew out to join me. We traveled north to Redding, where he had spent his early childhood, and from there we went to San Anselmo to visit the seminary campus we hadn't seen since our graduation.

On campus I was awestruck once again by the idyllic setting, just as I had been twenty-one years earlier when I had first arrived. So much in my life had changed since then. Not only Tricia's death but the unfolding of my spiritual life in the wake of it, which had left me alienated from the religious tradition that had first brought me here.

The campus had changed as well. The historic stone buildings that had been evacuated after the earthquake of 1989 had been repaired and reoccupied. Montgomery Chapel, which had been in complete disrepair during our time as students, had been renovated. It was warm and inviting, circular, with beautiful stained-glass windows depicting nature scenes. It felt so feminine, and I wondered whether my seminary experience might have been any different had we been worshiping there twice a week rather than in dark, austere Stuart Chapel with its long, angular design and rows of stained-glass windows, all depicting men.

Since the last time I was on campus a labyrinth had been installed on the terrace that overlooked the valley in front of Mt. Tamalpais, and when evening came I walked it.

Over the years, the single winding path of the many labyrinths I had walked had been such a constant companion and teacher for me. I had learned to trust the twists and turns, knowing that they always managed, eventually, to lead me to the center. If I followed where the path led, I knew I would never get lost.

When I came at last into the center of the labyrinth and looked up at the white bell tower of Geneva Hall, set against the late-day sky, I sensed a profound blessing being offered to me that made me weep. I sensed I was being urged on in my journey, even if that journey took me beyond the Church. I could see that the Church wasn't a destination; it was a placenta. Its purpose was to protect and nourish nascent spiritual life until it was ready to be birthed into a new reality.

Once again, just as I had in the canyon, I felt something had changed within me. A chapter of my life was closing, though what that meant, exactly, I didn't yet know.

When we left California, Kip and I flew to Colorado to attend a weeklong retreat led by Thich Nhat Hanh. I had been looking forward to the retreat for months, eager to be in Thich Nhat Hanh's presence. He was someone I had long admired; with a quiet, humble demeanor, he taught that mindfulness and peace were practices that can be cultivated in every moment and every act of living.

From the Denver airport, Kip and I caught a chartered bus that took us up into the mountains. Driving past meadows where herds of elk grazed, surrounded by breathtaking peaks rising up against the clear Colorado sky, I felt overjoyed to be back home again.

We arrived at the YMCA in Estes Park. Once we got settled into our room, we headed for the convocation hall to attend the opening gathering. There, a thousand other people who had traveled from far and wide were convening and taking their seats on the floor. Kip and I joined them and waited expectantly for Thich Nhat Hanh to come onstage and begin the opening talk.

After everyone had settled, one of the brown-robed monks approached the microphone on stage and began to read a letter from Thay (as Thich Nhat Hanh is affectionately called). It was a beautiful, loving letter, but as he began to read it I was confused. Why was Thay communicating with us in writing rather than just addressing us in person? Was this the custom at the beginning of a Buddhist retreat?

Slowly, though, it sank in. Thich Nhat Hanh would not be joining us. He was hospitalized in Boston, receiving treatment for a serious lung infection. His community—nuns and monks who had traveled from France and from their sister monasteries in New York and California—would lead the retreat. They would give the dharma talks, lead us in our times of meditation, and facilitate our small group discussions.

When the monk finished reading the letter, a stunned silence filled the hall. The disappointment was palpable, as was the heavy concern for Thich Nhat Hanh's health.

As the reality of the situation sank in, I came to a reluctant acceptance. Perhaps this was the first teaching of this retreat: releasing my attachment to something I had been looking forward to for so long. The situation was what it was. There was nothing to be done but to open myself to what it would offer. And after all, wasn't it a mistake to project onto a single leader the spiritual potentials we all hold?

The nuns and monks did a beautiful job. They gave insightful, moving dharma talks sprinkled with abundant humor. Although I'm sure they felt anxious about having to fill Thay's shoes, their sincerity, the depth of their presence, and the authenticity of their teaching was inspiring.

Over the week we coalesced into a supportive community, meditating together, sharing our meals in silence, joining in small group conversations, and accepting the situation with grace and humor. In the absence of the leader, the community discovered its own strength and wisdom.

As the retreat drew to a close, we all knew we had taken part in something extraordinary. An amazing transformation had taken place in the span of just a few days. Rather than an event where a thousand people gathered to absorb the wisdom of one Buddhist master, the retreat had released the wisdom of the *sangha* itself—not despite Thich Nhat Hanh's absence but because of it.

On our last evening we had a celebration, and each small group offered a skit or song, many of them ingeniously funny. One group presented a reading in the rhyming style of Dr. Seuss, with the continual refrain: "Thich Not Here."

The most extraordinary moment of the celebration, though, was when a spontaneous snake dance erupted as Michael Jackson's "Man in the Mirror" was played over the loud speakers. *If you wanna make the world a better place, take a look at yourself and make a change.* The hall was pulsing with ecstatic energy.

Thich Nhat Hanh's community would later christen the retreat the "miracle of the Rockies." To add to the wonder, the name of the retreat, which had been decided on months earlier, was "One Buddha Is Not Enough."

On the morning of our departure, when we gathered one last time in the convocation hall, our small group leaders handed out certificates to those of us who had received the Five Mindfulness Trainings—concrete practices intended to cultivate the Buddhist vision for a global spirituality and ethic. They emphasized reverence for life; true happiness; true love; loving speech and deep listening; and nourishment and healing. I appreciated how the trainings brought Buddhist teachings to life, and so I had participated in the ceremony and committed myself to practicing them.

As the nun who had been our small group leader was passing out our certificates, she gestured me aside. Once we were out of earshot of the others, she said softly, "When I was contemplating what your dharma name was to be, what I got was 'Living Christ of the Heart.' But I didn't know if you'd be able to use that name in the company of others, so what I wrote on your certificate is 'Joyful Gift of the Heart.' I want you to understand the name was *Living* Christ of the Heart. *Living.* It wasn't referring to someone or something in the past. It was a present reality. A *living* reality."

Later that morning, before we left for Denver to visit my mother, Kip and I took a hike. As we stood beside a mountain stream I thought about the dharma name the Sister had privately shared with me.

I didn't know what to make of it, and found it troubling. The term Christ—having been distorted by the ego mind to refer to a person rather than a consciousness—carried too many disturbing associations for me. I wanted nothing to do with it. Christianity no longer held true for me. After my trip to Israel even Jesus had become foreign to me. Throughout the retreat I had longed to understand the dharma of Jesus, which, it seemed to me, had been lost to centuries of the ego's convoluted interpretations. I felt I was moving away from that lineage altogether. And yet even here—at a Buddhist retreat—it seemed to be claiming me.

Chapter 29: The Winding Path

I tried to ignore the sound of the clicking shutter as I walked the labyrinth at Central Presbyterian in Denver. When I arrived, a photographer from *The Denver Post* had told me they were doing an article about an upcoming workshop about the labyrinth and asked if he could photograph me while I walked it. Having someone take pictures—for a newspaper, no less—of what for me was a very private act wasn't what I had bargained for, especially today, but I had agreed. Now he was up in the balcony, documenting the moment.

I had come to the labyrinth desperate for guidance. I was in Denver to be with my mother. A cancer she had had a few years before had returned, and the previous summer her doctor had given her just a few months to live. But it wasn't only the impending loss of my mother that was weighing on me. I knew now that I had to leave Tabernacle.

After Kip's and my trip to California and our retreat in Colorado, on the first morning I returned to work, I stood at my office door fumbling with the lock. It was so strange. I had had the same key for twelve years and it had never given me any trouble before.

When I finally got the door unlocked, I opened it onto a jarring sight. Several of my bookshelves had been emptied—the books stacked on the floor—and the framed photographs of former pastors going back to the church's founding in the 1880s had been pulled out of the corner, where they had been gathering dust for years, and were leaning up against the sofa.

The office looked like it was being packed up and the former pastors had come out of their hiding place to invite me to join their ranks.

It's time for me to go, I thought, stunned by the sight.

I soon found out that the "real" reason the books and portraits had been moved was that there had been a water leak in the roof while I was away and our office manager had moved them so they wouldn't get damaged. The fact that my key no longer wanted to work remained a mystery.

Just as unsettling, I found it exceedingly difficult to reengage with my work. It was as though a chasm had opened up between me and the pastoral role. I simply couldn't muster the energy to bridge it.

When I had been in California and sensed that a chapter in my life was closing, it seems I hadn't been imagining things. I just hadn't expected it to happen so quickly.

I had always trusted I would know when it was time for me to leave Tab. A part of me thought I might stay there until I retired. But a few months before my trip to California, I had begun having dreams suggesting that the time for my departure might be approaching.

In one dream I was standing in the prayer circle with the congregation during worship when a breeze came through an open window and blew out the oil lamp on the communion table. I tried several times to relight it, but couldn't.

The following night I had a dream in which I stepped out of the church at night. The sky was filled with stars, and I was looking up at two constellations I recognized: the

Cross and the Crown. Suddenly the entire sky shifted and the constellations plummeted to the horizon.

A couple nights later I had yet another dream in which I was in the sanctuary looking for the large crystal prayer bowl we always played at the beginning of worship, but I couldn't find it. All I found underneath the communion table was a Styrofoam bowl filled with Styrofoam packing peanuts.

But the dream that had haunted me the most featured Jean-Luc Picard, captain of the Enterprise on *Star Trek: The Next Generation.*

Kip and I were Trekkies, and I had always found the character of Picard to be especially compelling. He was an exemplary captain who led his crew with wisdom, courage, and integrity.

In the dream I was shown the place in outer space where Picard was going die (or had died, it wasn't clear which), chained to a stone, arch-like structure, exposed to outer space. There was no indication that his death was the result of malice. It seemed he had offered himself willingly. But his death was tragic because nothing had been gained by it. It had been an empty, unnecessary sacrifice with no redemptive purpose.

The dream troubled me. In the television series, the Starship Enterprise's mission was "to boldly go where no one has gone before." I had come to hear it as: "to boldly go where No One has gone before." It seemed the dream was warning me that the spiritual explorer in me that sought to leave behind the ego's illusions and boldly explore the Reality of No One was in danger of dying. But to understand the dream fully I needed to know what the stone structure Jean Luc had been chained to represented.

Then it came to me. The object in waking life that most resembled what I had seen in the dream was a stone stained-glass window frame at church. Chained to the structure of the church and its thought system, the spiritual explorer in me would die. Even worse, nothing would be gained by the sacrifice. It would be empty—devoid of any redemptive value.

The signs were becoming increasingly clear that it was time for me to resign, and yet I needed to sit with this knowing to see if it persisted. Tabernacle had been my spiritual home for twelve years. It was a beloved community of kindred spirits, and once I left I wouldn't be able to return. The mere thought of leaving filled me with grief.

It was late August 2009 when I returned from California. I decided to wait until the New Year, and if by then I still strongly sensed it was time for me to leave, I would submit my resignation.

A month after our return, Kip and I attended a memorial service for Thomas Berry at the cathedral of St. John the Divine in New York City. Berry, a Catholic priest and self-proclaimed geologian, was a thought leader in the "New Story" movement, which wedded the insights of evolutionary science, cosmology, and spirituality.

The service was magnificent. The pipe organ accompanied Paul Winter on saxophone as Wangari Maathai, Brian Swimme, Sister Miriam Therese MacGillis, and others processed to the front of the chancel to lead the service.

Even though I hadn't known of his work at the time, so much of what Berry had said resonated with the insights that had come to me in the spiritual opening I had experienced years earlier. Like Teilhard de Chardin before him, Berry could sense that the entire Universe was evolving into greater and greater consciousness, and he understood that story would determine our evolutionary path.

In this age of mass extinction—the result of humans'

alienation from the Earth—Berry had called for a new human species, one aware of its oneness with all of life and living out a generative, mutually-enhancing relationship with the Earth. Simply, he was asking us to transform our story from one of alienation and destruction into one of mutuality and wonder.

I was grateful to be present at this celebration of Berry's life, and relieved to be among so many kindred spirits.

That fall I gave a series of sermons I titled *The Second Coming of Christianity*, in which I put forth my vision of what a future Christianity might look like. I talked about how we will no longer conceive of God as the Holy One, external to ourselves, but as the Wholly One, a living Reality that includes us and in which we are active co-creators.

How Jesus will no longer be seen as an exception to humanity, a God-Man come to save us, but someone who revealed our own true nature, freed from the ego and its illusions.

We will understand that the cruelties we have inflicted on one another and the Earth are not evidence of our depravity but the inevitable outcome of a consciousness not yet aware of the unified nature of Reality.

A transformed Christianity will proclaim that all beings and all matter participate in the Incarnation and are infused with the consciousness that pervades all Reality.

We will no longer see the crucifixion as an atoning sacrifice reconciling humanity to an external God but as Jesus's demonstration of the unreality of judgment and death.

Nor will we wait for the Second Coming. We will participate in it, opening ourselves to the same consciousness Jesus experienced, unleashing our divine capacities to heal the world. I concluded the series saying, "*We* are the Christ we've been waiting for."

The series was my manifesto. The following week, I

left Philadelphia for Denver to spend Thanksgiving with my family, the last we would have with my mother.

After the holiday was over and it was time for me to return home, I couldn't bear the thought of leaving my mother to contend with her pain and dwindling energy by herself, waiting alone in her condominium to die. I told her I would ask for a leave of absence from the church and stay with her, and for once my mother, who had always been fiercely independent, didn't argue with me. In fact, she seemed greatly relieved.

The church leadership granted my leave of absence without hesitation, and in the following weeks, with the help of my mother's hospice nurse, we got her pain and nausea under control.

A couple weeks after Thanksgiving I received an e-mail from the woman who was covering for me at the church, updating me on a few things. One thing she mentioned was that the Tab can on my desk had started leaking. She'd had to pour out the contents and had put the empty can back on my desk.

For me this news was the final confirmation that my intuitions had been correct. I had always somehow felt that that Tab can—a symbol of the deep connection I felt with the congregation—would indicate when it was time for me to go.

My mother had a rare form of cancer that was difficult to predict. Her doctor had told us the tumors that were growing in her abdomen, which had gotten quite large, would lead to a sudden intestinal rupture or blockage and she would experience a very rapid, final decline—but we had no way of knowing for sure when that might happen. All we had to go on was the doctor's prognosis and my mother's strong sense that it would not be long now.

She had just turned eighty-eight and was more than eager for "the good Lord" to take her, confident that "He" wouldn't make her wait. But as the weeks passed she became increasingly disheartened, and by the time the New Year rolled around she was despondent.

My own angst was intensifying as well. I didn't want to leave her, but my responsibilities to my congregation were also weighing on me. I was feeling increasingly uneasy about what was becoming an extended time away, especially knowing that when I returned I would be submitting my resignation.

Yet I also knew that once I submitted my resignation I would be committing myself to staying in Philadelphia for several weeks in order to bring my ministry to a close. If Mom's condition took a turn during that time I wouldn't be able to come back to Denver to be with her. My anxiety was further heightened by the fact that I hadn't told my mother I was going to resign. I feared it would upset her, and I didn't want her to spend her final days worrying about me.

This is what I struggled with that day at Central Presbyterian. I couldn't believe I was facing these two monumental losses at the same time. I tried to focus my attention on the labyrinth. In this moment it was my teacher, taking me first one way, then turning me around to walk in the opposite direction.

Life is not linear. Just follow the path.

I placed one foot in front of the other, over and over, as the labyrinth led me along its twisted path, surrendering myself to the turns my life was taking and saying an inward "yes" to the unknown future before me.

When I finally got to the center I knelt down to touch my forehead to the floor, to convey with my body that I was willing to walk this path and trust the spiritual realm to lead me.

A couple days later, a large photograph of me kneeling in the center of the labyrinth appeared on the front page of the newspaper, a jarringly public display of my moment of surrender. Equally jarring was that the accompanying article spoke of me as a Philadelphian. I had always seen myself as a Denver native, no matter where I lived. Now it seemed I was being exiled even from my home town.

Chapter 30: Loss of the Mother

Keeping my impending resignation a secret from my mother had finally become unbearable. Not long after my labyrinth walk, while Mom and I were sitting together at her dining room table, I began the conversation I had been dreading.

"There's something I've been wanting to tell you," I told her. "In the last few months I've realized that it's time for me to leave Tab."

She looked shocked. Her eyes got watery. "What will be next for you?"

"I'm not sure, but I'll probably be doing some writing."

She didn't probe, for which I was grateful. Nor did she try to dissuade me, which was something I cherished about her. Almost without exception she had always honored my decisions, letting me lead my own life. My fear hadn't been that she would try to talk me out of leaving the church, but that my departure would worry her in her final days. If it did, she didn't let on.

I felt relieved to have it all out in the open. Meanwhile,

Mom was undergoing her own surrendering, finally accepting the fact that this dying process would take however long it took. Her despair lifted and she took on a lightness of spirit that was beautiful to behold.

Tab's council had voted to extend my leave of absence, and in those few months I spent in Denver, we had the chance to be together in ways we never had before. She spoke about what she expected to experience after she died, and she shared some things about her growing-up years she had never talked about.

By the end of March Mom's condition remained unchanged. Her medications were keeping her pain and nausea under control, and I knew I had to return to Philadelphia to bring my ministry to a close. I just had to hope her final decline wouldn't happen while I was caught up in the intense conclusion of my work there. I made arrangements with her neighbors and with a hospice nurse who lived in her building; they assured me they would be available for her as needed.

On the day of my departure, Mom and I stood at the open door of her condominium, tears filling our eyes.

"Good-bye, Mom."

"Good-bye, dear. Call me when you get home."

"I will. I love you very much."

"I know you do. I love you too, dear."

We gave each other a long hug, knowing it might be our last, and then I left to catch my ride to the airport.

My first Sunday back at Tab the people were overjoyed to see me, and they even had a welcome-back ritual for me during worship. But two days later I met with the council and explained to them, weeping, that the time had come for me to resign.

When I finished speaking they were silent, in shock. Some got teary-eyed, others felt angry and betrayed.

We decided that my last Sunday would be Pentecost Sunday, giving me six weeks to go through my files, clear out my office, help the congregation prepare for the interim period, and meet with people individually and in small groups to try to help them understand the reasons for my resignation. At my going-away party, I bequeathed the Tab can to the congregation and told them how it had emptied out its contents while I was in Denver.

I felt such heaviness of heart. Since the time of my opening in the woods eight years earlier, I had always wondered whether the transformed Christianity I sensed was on the horizon could find its expression at Tabernacle. I had always hoped so, and yet now I knew it wasn't meant to be. Once again, dreams came to help me understand why.

This had been my journey, not Tabernacle's. It wasn't my place to impose my beliefs on them, which by now were far outside the mainstream. Progressive though Tab was, it was still part of the institutional church, which had its own architecture of belief. I would be jeopardizing the well-being of the community if I stayed, possibly dragging them into ecclesiastical conflicts over orthodoxy or causing a rift in the congregation between those eager for new perspectives and those who might resist them.

And even if they had wanted to join me in the exploration "to boldly go where No One had gone before," where would it have left them when I did finally leave and they had to find my successor? I had seen other churches go through painful tumult when long-tenured, beloved pastors who had shaped the community around their own theology and personality left. I didn't want Tabernacle to face that kind of hardship.

My final Sunday came. During worship we exchanged gifts, tears, prayers, and blessings. Afterward, during the fellowship time, person after person told me how much I had meant to them and how much they would miss me.

When the last stragglers left, the church was silent and empty. I broke down sobbing, spent from the emotional intensity of the last months and especially this final farewell.

Sara had stayed behind with me. "Are you okay?" she asked.

I shook my head. "I'm so exhausted."

"I can understand why. This has been so intense."

She put her hands on my back and did some energy work for me. After I had recovered a bit we headed out to meet some friends for brunch.

I opened the door and stepped outside. It was a gorgeous May afternoon. Acutely aware that I no longer had a key to the church and wouldn't be able to return, I pushed the heavy wooden door shut behind me until it locked in place. Then I walked away.

Over the next few months I traveled back and forth between Denver and Philadelphia as my mother worsened and then rebounded again. It wasn't until late October that her precipitous decline began, and ironically, I wasn't there.

Kip and I had just returned home from his college reunion in Rochester, New York when I got the call from my oldest brother, who lived in Colorado. My other brother, who lived in Omaha, took the overnight train. I booked a flight from Philly for the next day.

My brother and I stayed in her condominium with Mom, taking turns with the nursing duties. I took the morning shift.

"Mom? It's time for your medicine." Dawn was breaking outside her window.

She half-opened her glassy eyes and parted her lips slightly. I put the tip of the syringe in her mouth and slowly pushed the plunger until it was empty.

These final weeks had been painful and messy, not at all the gentle journey she had hoped the good Lord would give her. I wondered if it was taking a toll on her faith, which had always been so strong.

"I'm so sorry you're going through all of this," I said, putting my hand on her shoulder. "Are you angry with God that this is taking so long?"

She shook her head weakly and closed her eyes again.

On an early November morning, nearly a year after we had expected her to go, with my two brothers and me sitting vigil at her bedside, Mom quietly died.

As long as my mother was alive I had always felt I had a place I could go if I needed one, and during my dark night her love for me had been the only thing I had been sure of.

The Church, in many ways, had also been a mother to me. It had given me a place of belonging. It had nurtured me, launched me on my spiritual path, provided me a story to guide my way, called forth gifts in me I didn't even know I had.

Now, within the space of less than six months, I had lost them both.

Days after my mother died, I flew to Northern Ireland—my airfare having been Mom's parting birthday gift to me— to visit my friend Teya. Teya had been working in Northern Ireland for a couple of years, and while I was with my mother she and I had often synchronized our meditation times, feeling our connection despite the distance.

I took a red-eye flight from Philadelphia. Teya met me at the airport in Belfast, where we had a joyful reunion, and then she drove me to her flat in Derry, which overlooked the Foyle River.

We were sitting at her kitchen table having a cup of tea when she said, laughing, "Patricia, I have to say that I have never seen anyone look quite as exhausted as you do in this moment. I just *have* to take a picture!" She picked up her phone, took a picture, and showed it to me.

She was right. I did look exhausted.

Then she got serious. "I know you're in a threshold time. This is a very sacred time for you, so you just tell me what you need."

"Thank you. I will."

Teya was in Northern Ireland to help the people there heal from the Troubles using a process she had created called Theater of Witness. She listened to the experiences of both Catholics and Protestants, ex-combatants and victims, and from their stories created theater pieces in which the people themselves played their own parts.

I had planned my trip to coincide with performances of Teya's latest piece, *I Once Knew a Girl*, featuring an all-women cast. Acting their own parts, the women told their stories. One woman told of the night her husband Paddy was blown up by the IRA. Another woman told of her experience being a gun and ammunitions runner for the IRA.

That these people, who had been so traumatized and steeped in hatred, could come together, reconcile, and create a theater piece together was miraculous enough. But just as moving was seeing the audiences' reactions. Everyone attending the play had been touched by the Troubles in some way, and at the end of each performance they would be on their feet, tears streaming down their faces, applauding. They had just seen their personal and collective stories of violence and hatred transformed into a story of hope and reconciliation. They could see that it really was possible. We really did have the power to set the future free.

I felt so honored to be able to experience the work Teya had done there, and so grateful to my mother for having made my trip possible.

After leaving Tab I felt a mixture of grief, freedom, and fear. For the first time in my life I had no structure to hold me, no role or social standing, no spiritual community, no setting in which to offer my gifts, no clear direction. I desperately wanted to figure out what my future was to be, and at times felt as though life had led me to a dead end. But I finally realized the future wasn't something to be figured out. It was something to be lived into.

In the fall of 2011, a year after Mom died, I drove from Philadelphia to Colorado to join my family in scattering her ashes. To pass the time on the road I listened to some podcasts of Krista Tippet's radio show, *On Being*. Somewhere along the interstate going through Ohio, listening to an interview Krista did with a man who had made a documentary about Dietrich Bonhoeffer, I received a message—much like those that had come to me from time to time on retreat—delivered with the usual calm, dispassionate clarity, along with a firm sense of purpose. I would write a book called *Beyond Jesus* that would talk about how ego consciousness had shaped Christian belief.

Chapter 31: Beginning Again

The only way I could imagine writing the book I knew I was to write was by telling the story of my own journey, which had led me to see how Christianity had been shaped by the ego mind. The following summer I flew out to California to write, staying with a friend who lived in Point Reyes.

While I was there, Kip flew out and we spent a week of vacation together, revisiting some of the places we had frequented in seminary, including the area where we had spent our honeymoon. Early in the morning on the day of his departure, I took him to the bus station in East Marin so he could catch his flight back home.

I had offered to pick up my friend's computer, which was in for repairs, while I was in East Marin. Since the store wouldn't open for a few hours, I decided to walk the labyrinth at the seminary before getting some breakfast.

I got to the labyrinth just before sunrise. As the sun began to come up over the Marin Hills, I walked and thought about a hike I had recently taken on the Earthquake Trail

along the San Andreas Fault at Point Reyes National Sea-
shore. The trail took me past a fence that had been sheared
apart in the earthquake of 1906. I thought about how the
narrative of my life had been just as abruptly severed after
Tricia died. Giving myself over to the quest to discover the
essence of my existence, I had experienced a shattering realization of this world as a dream generated by the illusory
ego. With that realization I also saw how the religion of my
upbringing had been shaped by that very illusion.

And yet even though I had seen ego's influence on that
religion and had left my vocation in the Church, Christianity was still in my bones. I could no more excise the gospel stories from my mind than I could excise the vertebrae
of my spine. I continued to believe that there was wisdom
at the heart of Jesus's teaching that the planet—groaning
under the yoke of ego and its empires—needed now more
than ever.

Shortly after leaving Tab, I attended a concert at a
church in Center City Philadelphia. On the back wall of the
chancel behind the choir was a mural of the nativity: Joseph
and Mary kneeling beside the infant Jesus, who was lying in
a manger. Nearby were a donkey and a cow, and off to the
right the magi. But the only figures in the mural with halos
around their heads were Mary, Joseph, and Jesus.

There's the problem, I thought, pondering the implicit
message of the mural. It depicted the very belief that needed
to be transformed: that humans alone carry the divine light,
and only certain humans at that. *Imagine what would happen,* I
thought, *if churches all over the world hired artists to correct the religious iconography.* The artists' instructions would be to "no"
no one, to paint halos on all the humans, all the cows, don-
keys, sheep, trees—even the land itself. I had no doubt that
such iconography would help us begin to awaken from our
dream of separateness.

Although I had been unsuccessful in my attempt to bridge the gap between the tradition and what I had come to understand, I still believed there must be a way. I asked the labyrinth to show me how. No answer arose.

It was still early in the morning when I finished getting my breakfast. Since it was Sunday I decided to drive to Marin City to attend a church, St. Andrew, I had occasionally visited while in seminary. On my way there I thought back to a dream I had had a couple of months before leaving for California:

> *I am back in Israel, standing next to a large lake. I understand that this return visit to Israel will be the way Beyond Jesus will end. Although I am standing on the ground, I am simultaneously able to see the land from above. I can see that there are two rivers that flow into the lake from opposite shores. I'm standing next to one of them. I know this is where Jesus was crucified. I can still feel the energetic residue of the event lingering here.*
>
> *Now I am on the opposite side of the lake, in what seems to be an underground chamber through which the other river flows before emptying into the lake. The chamber is reminiscent of a cloister or a catacomb. There is a woman dressed in a white gown who has just undergone a ritual ceremony. During the ceremony she had a profound experience she is reluctant to speak about. Finally, I persuade her.*
>
> *She tells me that during the ritual, "Jesus streaked through, and others saw him as well." She uses the word "streaked" intentionally. He was naked. And as she says this I see a naked form, ethereal, not fully in the material realm, run past.*

Jesus, I'm then told, was the guru given me by the circumstances of my birth. I am shown a woman in India praying with her prayer beads, and I am given to understand that, just as she was assigned a guru by nature of the circumstances of her birth, so was I.

Large, dark, penetrating eyes then appear directly before me—Jesus's eyes—looking deeply, steadily into my own.

After so many years of struggling to understand my relationship with Christianity and Jesus, the dream came as a denouement. Despite our differences in culture, religion, geography and time, I was connected with Jesus because I had been born into a Christian family. But he wasn't my Lord and Savior, nor was he the one and only Son of God. He was my guru.

Having transcended the illusion of ego and its drives, an authentic guru never seeks to be worshipped or adored. A guru only seeks to liberate others from their illusions so they too can recognize their true nature—a nature they and their guru share—and experience their union with the loving Reality from which they came.

The lake had two shores. One was the shore of the illusory ego, its cruelties and crucifixions, its dream. The other was the shore of transformation, of awakening to my true nature.

The dream helped me see my error when, on my trip to Israel, I had allowed cultural and religious differences to alienate me from Jesus. Religion and culture belong to this temporal world. The world of empires and crucifixions. The world of our collective dream.

The historical, embodied Jesus who participated in a particular religion and culture had been crucified. But death exists only on the shore of our illusory dream. The true Self, one with the Ultimate, can never be destroyed. For it, neither time nor death exists. The awakened consciousness that had found expression in the human Jesus endured, and assisted still in the awakening of the willing. Perhaps that consciousness was what had been guiding me on my journey all along.

As I pulled off at the exit for St. Andrew, I thought again about a walk I had taken a few days before on the beach. It was a clear day, late afternoon. I was walking barefoot along the edge of the surf, watching the waves, the seagulls, the wet sand sparkling in the late-day sun.

Suddenly I felt as though I was looking *through* the eyes I had seen in my dream, seeing the world the way they saw it. I could see the miracle of everything around me. I could see how all things were shimmering with a Love that was almost too brilliant to bear. These were the eyes through which I now wanted to behold the world.

I got to St. Andrew a few minutes before worship began and sat down in the sanctuary. My attention was drawn to a large wooden cross hanging on the front wall. It was nagging at me, as though it had something to say about the question I had posed in the labyrinth about how to bridge the Christian tradition and the living Reality I had witnessed, but I wasn't sure why.

It wasn't until after worship was over and I was driving up Highway 101 that the pieces came together. It had been there all along in Christianity's central symbol: the cross. But the cross wasn't a symbol of judgment or punishment. It had nothing to do with a sacrifice to appease a righteous God. It was not a symbol of human cruelty being overcome by the power of divine love, as I had once thought.

Taking up one's cross meant relinquishing the illusions of ego: separateness and fear; the need to be special and to dominate; the belief in judgment, condemnation, and death.

If Christianity were to take up its own cross—releasing its need to be set apart and special, its need to survive, its projection of divinity onto a single Messiah—it would shapeshift from a religion worshiping a solitary Christ into a movement awakening us to the Christ Mind within us all.

I turned off the highway at Corte Madera, parked in the shopping mall lot, and headed for the store to pick up my friend's computer. It was a gorgeous day, and the outdoor mall with its flower planters and sidewalk cafes sparkled in the midday sunlight.

I had just gone past the store in search of a restroom when a woman walked past me going the other direction. My heart stopped. *Did I just see who I thought I saw?*

The woman looked just like Flora, my first-year roommate in seminary.

But it couldn't be Flora. She lived in Jakarta, Indonesia, where she was a pastor. She had come to California to work on her Doctor of Ministry degree the year we lived together, then returned to Indonesia. I hadn't seen or heard from her since, and that had been twenty-three years ago.

There was one way to find out if it was her. I stopped, turned around and called out, "Flora!"

The woman kept walking, in step with the young couple next to her.

"Flora!!"

The woman stopped and turned around. It was her.

It took a moment for her to recognize me, but when she did, her face lit up.

"Are you living in the US now?" I asked.

"No, no," she said, shaking her head. "I still live in Jakarta. I'm retired now! I'm visiting my son and his wife." She gestured to the young couple with her. "They live in East Bay." Her English had gotten a bit rusty.

"We thought we would bring her over to Marin for the afternoon," her son said, "since it's where she went to seminary. We thought she would enjoy seeing it again."

"Do you live here?" Flora asked me.

"No. I live in Philadelphia now."

"Philadelphia!" She clapped her hands together.

"Yes. I'm staying with a friend in Point Reyes. I'm also in East Marin just for the day!"

We all laughed, amazed at the impossible coincidence.

There is an ancient story that tells of a time when humans lived in the unmediated experience of the Source of Love, until we ate of the fruit of dualism and judgment. Self-consciousness arose. The ego was born and our long dream of separation, shame, and struggle began, a dream in which we seemed to need a Savior who could redeem us from our failures and reconcile us to a distant God. But the story also says there was another tree in the garden, a tree of life that could open our eyes to our immortality and awaken us to our divine nature.

Flora's remarkable appearance suggested that my education was about to start all over again, guided by a guru who knew the way back to the garden.

The four of us visited for a while, and then parted company. As I walked away I heard a woman behind me say, "Where *is* that damn Apple store?"

I stopped, turned around, and pointed. "It's that way, on the left."

She laughed and said, "I was talking to myself, but thank you."

I turned and walked on, laughing out loud in amazement at the Love that was flooding my being, unveiling the shimmering sentience all around me, stirring me from my dream.

Acknowledgments

This story would not be complete without expressing my deepest gratitude to those who have accompanied me on this journey and whose support and love have played a key role in my own becoming. Truly, I am because We are.

To my soul sisters Tricia Dietrich, Susan Teegen, Sara Steele, Teya Sepinuck, Lawrie Hartt, and Abby Stamelman-Hocky—dream workers, story weavers, shamans, mystics, artists. Your presence in my life gave me the courage to open to the Great Mystery and trust where it was leading me.

To Kip, my life companion, partner in the mundane and sublime, and occasional worthy opponent, I love you. Thank you for being your eccentric, poetic, playful self. Thank you for hanging in there when my life was unraveling and I couldn't see the way forward. Thank you for putting bread on the table and a roof over our heads during my wilderness years. Shine, live long, and prosper.

To Sue Westfall, Gwen Morgan, Zoana Gepner-Mueller, Patty Sundberg, Barb Nielsen, Marlene Skrobak, Sheila Weinberg, Bo Bartlett, Christine Lafuente, and so many others who have touched my life. Thank you for being my role models, healers, confidants, companions, and friends.

To my parents, Lois Pearce and Michael Pearce, whose love and support gave me a firm foundation, and whose quiet faith shaped me in ways I will never begin to know. Thank you also to my brothers, Mick and Ed, for being family, in the best sense of that word.

To the people of Central Presbyterian Church, who from the moment I was born welcomed me into the circle of your care, set me upon my spiritual journey, and supported my call to the ministry, my deepest appreciation. To the people of First Christian Church and Butler Presbyterian Church, thank you for providing me a place to grow. To the people of Tabernacle United Church, thank you from the depths of my heart for being my beloved community for so many years, for encouraging me in my spiritual explorations, and for being an unwitting anchor in my time of tumult. You will never know how much you mean to me.

To those who helped bring this book to life, my sincere thanks. To Deena Metzger, who encouraged me to tell this story openly rather than couch it in a work of fiction. To Myn Adess, who so generously provided me a quiet place with a wonderful view to dive into my writing. To David Colin-Carr, whose seasoned guidance and fierce editing helped bring shape and focus to a sprawling original manuscript. To Bob Tipton, whose enthusiasm for this book fortified my own belief. To my publisher, Brooke Warner, for trailblazing a path through the present upheavals in the publishing industry, and to Cait Levin, Krissa Lagos, and the editorial team at She Writes Press for all you are doing to amplify the voices and bring forth the experiences of women.

Finally, my heartfelt gratitude goes to you, the reader. If my journey has taught me anything it is that Reality is an intricate, interacting web of Being, which means my life has been touched by every life, including yours. Thank you for being on the planet at this auspicious moment of our evolution. Peace, joy, and courage to us all.

About the Author

Patricia Pearce was born and raised in Denver, Colorado. After graduating from the University of Colorado, she served as a Peace Corps Volunteer in the Andes of Ecuador. Her experience there set her on a path of spiritual exploration that took her into ordained ministry, and for seventeen years she served as a Presbyterian pastor. But in 2002, following the death of a close friend, she experienced a spiritual awakening that led her beyond the bounds of conventional Christian belief. She resigned from parish ministry in 2010 to embark on a vocation of writing, speaking, and teaching. She lives with her spouse in Philadelphia. Learn more about her work and download a free study guide for *Beyond Jesus* at www.patriciapearce.com.

Author photo © Conrad Louis-Charles

SELECTED TITLES FROM SHE WRITES PRESS

She Writes Press is an independent publishing company founded to serve women writers everywhere. Visit us at www.shewritespress.com.

Uncovered: How I Left Hassidic Life and Finally Came Home by Leah Lax. $16.95, 978-1-63152-995-5. Drawn in their offers of refuge from her troubled family and promises of eternal love, Leah Lax becomes a Hassidic Jew—but ultimately, as a forty-something woman, comes to reject everything she has lived for three decades in order to be who she truly is.

This Trip Will Change Your Life: A Shaman's Story of Spirit Evolution by Jennifer B. Monahan. $16.95, 978-1-63152-111-9. One woman's inspirational story of finding her life purpose and the messages and training she received from the spirit world as she became a shamanic healer.

Renewable: One Woman's Search for Simplicity, Faithfulness, and Hope by Eileen Flanagan. $16.95, 978-1-63152-968-9. At age forty-nine, Eileen Flanagan had an aching feeling that she wasn't living up to her youthful ideals or potential, so she started trying to change the world—and in doing so, she found the courage to change her life.

Change Maker: How My Brother's Death Woke Up My Life by Rebecca Austill-Clausen. $16.95, 978-1-63152-130-0. Rebecca Austill-Clausen was workaholic businesswoman with no prior psychic experience when she discovered that she could talk with her dead brother, not to mention multiple other spirits—and a whole new world opened up to her.

Her Name Is Kaur: Sikh American Women Write About Love, Courage, and Faith edited by Meeta Kaur. $17.95, 978-1-938314-70-4. An eye-opening, multifaceted collection of essays by Sikh American women exploring the concept of love in the context of the modern landscape and influences that shape their lives.

Where Have I Been All My Life? A Journey Toward Love and Wholeness by Cheryl Rice. $16.95, 978-1-63152-917-7. Rice's universally relatable story of how her mother's sudden death launched her on a journey into the deepest parts of grief—and, ultimately, toward love and wholeness.